Church of St. Paul the Apostle

Sermons Preached at the Church of St. Paul the Apostle

New York, during the year 1861

Church of St. Paul the Apostle

Sermons Preached at the Church of St. Paul the Apostle
New York, during the year 1861

ISBN/EAN: 9783337116781

Printed in Europe, USA, Canada, Australia, Japan

Cover: Foto ©Lupo / pixelio.de

More available books at **www.hansebooks.com**

SERMONS,

PREACHED

AT THE

Church of St. Paul the Apostle,

NEW YORK.

DURING THE YEAR 1861.

NEW YORK:
VAN PARYS, HUGOT & HOWELL,
34 BEEKMAN STREET.
1861.

Entered according to **Act of Congress, in** the year 1861, by
VAN PARYS, HUGOT & HOWELL,
In the Clerk's Office of the District Court of the United States, for the Southern District of New York.

C. A. ALVORD, PRINTER.

PREFACE.

Some of those friends who listened to the sermons contained in this volume have expressed a desire to see them in print, and thought they would do good. This friendly counsel has not been acted upon without hesitation. The great scarcity of Catholic sermons in English would seem to afford motive enough for publishing, though it is feared that these may fall too far below the standard. Certainly, they make no pretence to brilliant passages of imagination, flowers of style, or appeals to popular enthusiasm; these not comporting with the serious and earnest work in which we are engaged. But we trust that they will be found plain, simple, and direct, and that there may be those among our Catholic brethren who will derive an appreciable benefit from their perusal—some clearer view of Christian doctrine or moral duty, some thought to touch the heart, and draw it upward to God. If so, our purpose will have been accomplished. With so much of explanation we send out these few sermons into the world; doubting, somewhat, if all who heard them when they came living and warm from the preacher's lips, and listened with interest then, will prize them now as they lie cold and uncolored on the paper.

St. Paul's, 59th Street. Dec. 1, 1861.

CONTENTS.

		PAGE.
I.	THE EARNEST MAN	9
II.	UNWORTHY COMMUNION	26
III.	CHRIST'S RESURRECTION THE FOUNDATION OF OUR FAITH	40
IV.	GIVING TESTIMONY	63
V.	SPIRITUAL DEATH	76
VI.	THE LOVE OF GOD	93
VII.	KEEPING THE LAW NOT IMPOSSIBLE	107
VIII.	THE TWO STANDARDS	124
IX.	THE EPIPHANY	143
X.	RENUNCIATION	158
XI.	THE AFFLICTIONS OF THE JUST	176
XII.	FALSE MAXIMS	190
XIII.	MARY'S DESTINY A TYPE OF OURS	205
XIV.	MORTAL SIN EXEMPLIFIED IN THE HISTORY OF JUDAS	221

		PAGE.
XV.	Interior Life	234
XVI.	True Christian Humility	254
XVII.	What the Desire to Love God can do	270
XVIII.	The Worth of the Soul	293
XIX.	Merit the Measure of Reward	310
XX.	Self-Denial	330

SERMON I.

THE EARNEST MAN.

A SERMON FOR THE COMMEMORATION OF ST. PAUL, APOSTLE.

(From the Epistle, Gal. i., 11-23.)

I HAVE read the Epistle for the day, rather than the Gospel, because it contains a brief but characteristic sketch of the great Apostle, drawn by his own hand. How strange is the history of this man! We have here the Church's most bitter persecutor converted into the most zealous and successful of all the Apostles. At first we discover a careful and devoted student of the Jewish law; afterward he stands forth the most learned and eloquent expounder of the Christian Gospel. We see him in his youth a witness of St. Stephen's martyrdom, standing by to hold the garments of those who stoned him to death, sternly and pitilessly looking on; and again in his old age we find him lying lifeless on the Ostian road, outside the walls of Rome, a headless trunk, a martyr in the same cause for which St. Stephen died. We see him at first "*ravaging the Church, entering into houses, and haling away men and women, and committing them to prison,*" and shortly afterward we hear the wondering Christians whisper to each other: "*He that persecuted us in times past now preaches the faith.*" In the beginning, foremost of all the Jews was he in that terrible energy which they put forth to destroy the Church; and afterward foremost among the Apostles, he was able to say with truth: "*I have labored more abundantly than they all.*" In fine, one trait of character distinguished this great Apostle at all times, both before and after his conversion. He was always an earnest man. It is worth our while this morning to study his character well, for—from the bottom of my soul I do believe it—a few such earnest Christians in our day would be enough to move the world.

Let us look at him first during the early part of his career, and see how this earnestness of character displays itself in one whose mind is misguided by religious error. In the first place, then, St. Paul before his conversion was distinguished by an earnest and ardent love of truth, and consequently, a strong attachment to what he deemed to be the truth. I have already read to you in the Epistle what he says of his own early life: "*I made progress in the Jews' religion above many of my equals in my own nation, being more abundantly zealous for the traditions of my fathers.*" This earnestness of his sprang from a deep love of truth, and it made him what he afterward became, the foremost champion of the true faith. The human mind is created for truth, is naturally attracted to the truth when fairly presented, and if not led away by a corrupted heart, embraces it with joy. Truth comes readily to those that love it, and therefore there is, after all, nothing unnatural in this conversion of a Hebrew zealot into a Christian evangelist; for if he loved error at first, it was only because in good faith he mistook it for the truth, and if he hated the truth, it was only because he did not see it in its true colors, but misrepresented and perverted. These men who are zealous, honestly zealous, in error, are the very men to embrace the truth; and, on the contrary, they who stand perfectly indifferent between contradictory creeds, are the least open to conviction. Both reason and experience teach this. Nothing is more common in our day than a class of men who look with perfect good nature upon every form of religious doctrine, except perhaps that particular one in which they themselves were reared, and which is supposed therefore to have some practical claim upon them. Did you ever know one of these "liberal fellows," so called, to become Catholic? I mean these men who, having no religious faith to love, can have no error to hate. I mean, for example, these nominal Protestants who, when in your presence, turn into ridicule every Protestant form of religion, without believing a word of yours; one of these good-natured fellows that think the Catholic religion is quite as good as any, in some respects the best of any, since it is the farthest out of their way. Take, for instance, one of these liberal politicians that you always see at the public dinner on Patrick's day; that will subscribe cordially to a Catholic charity, if you ask him, but comes back to remind you of it on election day. Did you ever know a man of this stamp to become Catholic? No, indeed; divine truth has attractions only for earnest souls. A *hickory* Protestant is as poor a thing as a *hickory* Catholic. Such a man has two fundamental axioms to get by heart, before religious truth can take possession of his soul; first, that there is such a thing as truth, and next, that his mind was made for it, and needs it. Oh! it is sad to see a man in ignorance of the way of salvation,—sadder still to see him blindly prejudiced against it; but the saddest, most ignoble, and most hopeless of all conditions, is to be indifferent to it.

St. Paul was another type of man. He was an earnest one. He believed the Jewish religion to be the true and only true one, and therefore he loved it with all his soul, and was zealous for it. When the scales fell from his eyes, and the Christian faith was revealed to him in all its truth and beauty, he embraced it, and clung to it, and abandoned himself to it, with all the energies of that same earnest soul. Had he been a "liberal" Jew, we should have far more reason to wonder at his conversion; it is still less probable that God would have selected him for the Apostle of the Gentiles.

An earnest lover of truth, even before his conversion, it followed as a natural consequence, that St. Paul hated error; and for this reason he opposed the Christian religion with all his might, and with his whole soul, because he believed it to be false and dangerous. "*You have heard,*" said he, writing to the Christians of Galatia, "*of my conversation in time past in the Jews' religion, how that beyond measure I persecuted the Church of God, and laid it waste.*" But he tells us elsewhere: "*I obtained mercy of God, because I did it ignorantly in unbelief.*" In the same proportion that the earnest man loves what is good and true, he hates what is false and evil, or what he thinks so, and opposes it too. St. Paul opposed the Christian faith with all his power, because he believed it to be false. He was wrong there: it was an error of judgment. He persecuted it too violently, "beyond measure," forgetting the rules of charity. There he was wrong again; it was an error of the heart. But in all this he was in earnest, hating false doctrine; and there he was right. I do not sympathize with his delusion, but I love him for his earnestness.

Oh! how many such men may there not be in this country of ours, that we rank among our bitterest foes!—men who honestly oppose our holy religion, not for what it really is, but what they think it to be. Could we open that sealed and sacred register of the divine counsels, wherein the fortunes of mankind are written, with what delight should we read there the names of many of our bitterest opponents who are destined to kneel and worship with us yet, as others, thank God, have done already! Why not? I do from my heart believe that many of these make war upon us only from mistake of judgment. They know our doctrines only by false report. They judge of our morals only by such Catholics as are either the most ignorant of their own religion, or else entirely false to the teachings of their Church, and strangers to her sacraments, although some of these may be loud enough at times in proclaiming a faith they have not, to further some political pretension, or sanctify some ungodly trade. Under such circumstances it is not strange that many earnest men should set their faces against us. Could they cease to hate our religion, while they believe it to be false? Can they sympathize with us, while they believe us to be corrupted by it? Oh! God, send these men into thy fold! Take off the scales from their eyes, and send them to us. We need earnest men amongst us. The half-hearted, indifferent Protestant who calls himself a liberal, we do not hope for. We have too many such already; we could spare them by the thousand, for they neither save their own souls, nor bring credit to thy cause. But send us earnest men like St. Paul, who know how to hate error, because they love the truth!

If, even when groping in the darkness of Judaism, St. Paul was so honest-hearted and earnest, we shall not find him otherwise when enlightened by the grace of Jesus Christ, and enlisted in his holy cause. He had before him two great enterprises, which require not only large grace from God, but all one's manhood and energy to carry on well. He had his own soul to sanctify and save, and he had an Apostle's work to do. He set about both like a man in earnest, with that deliberate, deep and concentrated enthusiasm which is not wont to fail. Let us see first what care he took of his own salvation.

Would you believe it, my brethren, that St. Paul—after all that wonderful life of toil and privation in the cause of Christ, after his many voyages and frequent shipwrecks, imprisoned often, and dragged before different tribunals, after being scourged five times by the Jews and three times by the Romans, stoned by the mob in the streets and left for dead, wandering about without any fixed home, and often famishing for food and drink, and faint for want of sleep—would you believe, I say, that he yet trembled for fear of being damned? He was afraid lest that poor, emaciated body of his might rebel against the spirit, and drag him into some grievous sin. "*Oh! wretched man that I am!*" was his mournful cry, "*who shall deliver me from this body of death?*" For this reason he scourged himself. "*Therefore I chastise my body, and bring it into subjection, lest, perhaps, when I have preached to*

others, I myself should become reprobate."
This is being in earnest. I think, my brethren, our bodies are as dangerous to us, as St. Paul's was to him. Are we as much in earnest to guard against a fall? Gluttony, drunkenness, impurity, idleness and effeminacy—these sensual sins are generated in the body. We may not, all of us, be guilty of them, not grossly guilty; but we are none of us quite safe against them. What means do we employ to subjugate our bodies, or was St. Paul less safe than we?

According to the idea of this great Apostle, the way to heaven is a constant and difficult warfare. Nothing in language can be more striking and vivid than his description of an earnest Christian struggling to make sure his salvation. He compares him to wrestlers, boxers, and runners in the public games. Have you ever seen two strong men wrestling? How their muscles harden into knots, and their veins swell full as if they would burst! How all their energies are engaged! How wary they are to guard against a fall, and how quick to seize upon any advantage! Imagine them to be real enemies wrestling for life, and then you have an image of the actual contest of an earnest Christian struggling for salvation with the enemies of his soul. "*Brethren*," says St. Paul, and I seem to hear those deep tones giving counsel like a friendly voice at the beginning of a deadly fray, "*Brethren, put on the armor of God, that you may be able to stand against the snares of the devil. For our wrestling is not against flesh and blood, but against principalities and powers, against the rulers of this world of darkness, against the spirits of wickedness in the high places.*" Tell me, my brethren, is this your idea of the Christian warfare? Is it with this terrible earnestness you struggle to work out your salvation, or do you make a pastime of it?

He compares us Christians to professional racers. "*Know you not that they who run in the race all run indeed, but one receiveth the prize? So run that you may win.*" For my part, he adds, "*I so run as not at an uncertainty,*" not as if I had lost sight of the mark, and were only half conscious of what I were about, but "*forgetting the things that are behind, and stretching myself forward to those that are before me, I pursue towards the mark, for the prize of the supernal vocation of God in Christ Jesus."* Is this the earnest way we follow out our vocation? Are we thus determined to win?

The Christian warfare requires careful preparation, drill and discipline. In respect to this, St. Paul compares us to professional boxers, and his description shows that these gladiators of the olden time took as much pride in their art, as our modern gentlemen of the prize ring. "*Every one that struggles in a combat, abstains from every indulgence; they, indeed, that they may receive a corruptible crown, but we an incorruptible.*" How earnest are these miserable prize-fighters after their belt, and their stakes! How patiently they submit to all the rules of their training-master during their long and painful course of training! What abstinence from food, from indulgence in drink, and all luxurious living, in order to reduce their bodies to the most athletic proportions! What long walks under heavy weights! What fatiguing exercises to harden their muscles! Oh! that we were half as earnest, with heaven for a prize, and all our eternity at stake! We should be sure of victory then. St. Paul was in earnest. "*I so fight,*" said he, "*as not having to beat the air, but I chastise my body, and bring it into subjection, lest, perhaps, when I have preached to others, I myself should become reprobate.*"

We have seen now, how, after his conversion, St. Paul set about the first great business before him—his own salvation. Let us look at him now as an Apostle, engaged in gaining souls to God, and in guarding the flock of Christ intrusted to him. Ah! my dear brethren, here must I be brief. I dare not make any further demands upon your patience. And, besides, who can draw the lineaments of that great Apostle, or paint him in colors worthy of his character? What memory can trace out those long and frequent journeys, with the incessant fatigue of preaching, disputing, and writing, with the "care of all the churches" upon his hands. And yet, not to burden his brethren, he maintained himself in good part by manual labor. What language is gentle enough, and warm enough, to represent that tender and sensitive heart that throbbed in sympathy with all the joys and woes of the Church, and burned with every scandal? "*Who is weak,*" said he, "*and I am not weak? Who is scandalized, and I do not burn?*" Who can estimate the depth and fulness of that fraternal love, which made him willing to part even with his own hopes of heaven, so it could be done without offence to God, in order to save his brethren? "*My conscience bears me witness in the Holy Ghost that I have great sadness, and continual sorrow in my heart, for I wished myself to be an anathema from Christ for my brethren.*" This is the nearest approach to the love of the Saviour for us, who bore our sins upon the bitter cross, who died that we might live, becoming an anathema for his brethren. Oh! holy zeal for souls! how beautiful it shows in the person of an Apostle like St. Paul! And what an example it is for those of us who are in the sacred ministry. We, too, have a share in his Apostleship; we are charged with the preaching of the Gospel, and the gathering in of souls. We have pledged ourselves to this holy work of duty and charity. Woe to such among us as are not in earnest! Joy to him who, when his Lord comes, shall be able to give a good account of his stewardship!

But you, my dear brethren, have also something to learn from this burning zeal of St. Paul's. You have all something to do with the advancement of your Master's kingdom, and the salvation of souls. When God created the human race, so we read in the Book of Ecclesiasticus, he made each man responsible, in some measure, for the welfare of his fellows: "*Mandavit illis unicuique de proximo suo.*" and there is still a closer and dearer bond which embraces all the members of the great Catholic Church, and holds each one pledged to labor for the salvation of all. Ah! brethren, do not say with the murderer Cain: "*Am I my brother's keeper?*" What have I to do with the sanctification or ruin of souls? No! no! but take to heart your Master's cause. He came into the world to save sinners. Teach your heart to throb in sympathy with his, until you can say with St. Paul: "*Who is weak, and I am not weak? who is scandalized, and I do not burn?*" This is to love our Lord in earnest. This is the communion of saints.

We have traced this distinguishing characteristic of the great apostle—this earnestness of his—through his entire career. It only remains now to witness the close of that career. St. Paul died like a man who had lived in earnest, and for whom therefore death has no terrors, "*For me to live,*" said he, "*is Christ, to die is gain.*" Is it possible that any fear of death, any doubt of his salvation could cloud the spirit of such a man in the closing scene of his career? Listen to his parting song of triumph! It comes from his prison at Rome, just upon the eve of his martyrdom. He has still before his mind's eye the combatants and runners in the public games. "*The time of my dissolution is at hand. I have fought a good fight, I have finished my course; I have kept the faith. For the rest there is laid up for me a crown of justice, which the Lord the just Judge will render to me at that day.*"

Could we say as much, my brethren, if our time were come? Could we claim as manfully to have fought a good fight? Could we claim our reward as confidently? No? Then, alas, we have not been so much in earnest. We have been playing with our salvation, not wrestling for it; we have not been fighting for our faith with the world and Satan, but compromising; we have been resting not running;

and if so, what hope have we to reach that crown? Oh, let us bestir ourselves! Let us live like men awake; so let us think, so speak, so act, so move, through this brief but solemn crisis of life, that all who see us may know that, like St. Paul, we are in earnest.

SERMON II.

UNWORTHY COMMUNION.

"He that eateth and drinketh unworthily, eateth and drinketh judgment to himself, not discerning the Body of the Lord."—1 Cor. xi., 29.

(From the Epistle for Thursday in Holy Week.)

It is customary at certain seasons of the year, for separated members of a family to meet and dine together, as a means of cherishing that affection for one another which we look for among relations. Thanksgiving Day and Christmas are occasions of this kind. The Catholic Church, too, is a great family, and the Paschal Season is such a time with her. She calls her children around her altars, to receive the Body and Blood of her Lord, who is the blessed bond of their union, and of their love. But as in the parable of the rich man's supper there was found one at the table who had not on the wedding garment, and was cast out; therefore the Church warns us at this season, to prepare for the Paschal Feast, that we may not be found unworthy. And to the same end she calls upon us to keep this season of penance, beforehand. In the Church's name, then, and in charity to yourselves, my dear brethren, I am going to lift up my voice this morning, against unworthy communions.

But first, I must tell you, that I do not mean unworthy, in the sense of communions made without profit: as for example, when one makes but little preparation beforehand, and thinks little of what he is doing at the moment, and makes but the poorest sort of thanksgiving afterward. No; compared with such as I mean, these communions are precious and holy. They do but little good to those who make them, it is true; and give but poor honor to God; but at least they are made in the state of grace. By an unworthy communion, I mean one that is made in known mortal sin. I mean a sacrilegious communion. I shall speak, then,—

1. Of communion in itself.
2. Of unworthy communions.
3. Of those who are guilty of them.

I.—*What is Communion?*

It is the Body and Blood of Jesus Christ, given to us as food for the sanctification of our souls and bodies. "*He that eateth my Flesh, and drinketh my Blood, hath everlasting life, and I will raise him up at the last day.*"*

What is Holy Communion? It is to receive the best of friends, who comes to advise us, to cheer and to encourage us. A friend who has power to protect us. Who loves to dwell in our hearts as in a castle, where He may fight for us against the enemies of our soul.

What is Holy Communion? It is a pledge of Heaven, and a foretaste of it. Union with God by a perfect love, will be our happiness for all eternity, and this is begun on earth in Holy Communion. As St. Peter says, it is to be made "partakers of the Divine nature."†

What is Holy Communion? It is the parting gift of one who loves us better than our mother. He chose the time when He

* St. John, vi., 55. † 2 Peter i., 4.

was about to leave us, to give it an additional value. He made it the memorial of His Passion. As in times past, He had given the rainbow as a perpetual remembrance of His mercy, so He willed that the Blessed Sacrament of His Body and Blood, should be a perpetual remembrance of the redemption of the Cross, "*Do this in remembrance of Me.*"

What is Holy Communion? It is the best of all the good gifts of our good God.

II.—*What then is it to receive this Holy Communion unworthily?* It is to be grievously wanting in reverence to the holiest of all holy things. When you see a person put a thing to an improper use, what do you say? Why, that is too bad; you say. Why, you must be out of your head. Suppose you saw a girl in service, scrubbing the floor with a beautiful camel's-hair shawl, what would you say? Suppose you saw me filling the water stoups at the door, and for that purpose dipping out the holy water, from a pail, with the very chalice I had just used in Mass, what would you say? Why, you would exclaim, how very shocking! what an irreverent Priest! Now why would you say this? Because when God made your soul, He put into it a reverence for certain things, above others. But what does an unworthy communion do? It does this. It takes the Blood of Christ, and pours it down a sink that is more loathsome than a city sewer, for what is so loathsome to God, as a soul in mortal sin? Corruption of matter is good, for God made it, but moral corruption is an abomination to Him.

This one does who conceals a mortal sin in confession.

What is an Unworthy Communion? It is to crucify Jesus over again. What does St. Paul say? "*They who have tasted of the Heavenly Gift and are fallen away, crucify to themselves the Son of God, and make a mockery of Him.*" Now, which is worse, to leave off keeping a man's company, or to play the false friend with him? But this a man does who receives Holy Communion unworthily. The spirit of his act is as if he went up to the throne of God, and caught hold of those Blessed Hands and Feet, and said, "come down to earth and be tormented once more." He would pull off the crown of glory from that

Blessed Head, and press down again upon that Brow the crown of thorns.

Nay, it does even worse than crucify Jesus over again. His first crucifixion was a willing one. It was His own love that was the real executioner; but now He is dragged against His will. This is what a man does who gets his absolution on the strength of some promise which he does not intend to keep.

What is an Unworthy Communion? It is to eat and drink one's own damnation. What does St. Paul say again? "*He that eateth and drinketh unworthily, eateth and drinketh judgment to himself.*" The wood of the cross drank in the Blood of Christ, and was sanctified; and here is a soul that has drunk it in, and is damned. The Centurion was sprinkled with it, as he was piercing the side of Christ with a spear, and it made a Saint of him; but here is a Christian soul, that is damned for being bathed with it. It cleansed the robber's conscience who was hanging beside his Lord, and pleaded mercy for him; but on this soul it cries for vengeance, like the blood of Abel, against another Cain. " *Better*," said our Lord, " *had it been for that man, if he had not been born;"* but now, he has anticipated the Day of Judgment upon himself. This a man does who gets his absolution upon the promise of breaking off from a bad companion, which promise he does not mean to keep. I repeat, then, they make unworthy, sacrilegious communions, for instance,

1. Who conceal mortal sins in confession.
2. Who get their absolution on the strength of their promising what they do not intend to perform.

But what am I saying? Surely no one before me has been guilty of this! Well, God only knows. It has been done elsewhere, and may have been done here, for alas, unworthy communions are not such very uncommon things. In case it has been so, I wish to strike terror into such consciences, and to bring them to penance. I wish to prevent such a misfortune, in the parish of St. Paul's, as one coming to the Paschal Feast of the Lamb without his wedding garment.

III.—*Who has done this?*

As our Lord sat at the table with His Apostles, at the Last Supper, he said sadly, "*One of you shall betray Me.*" Each in turn, asked Him eagerly and earnestly, "*Lord, is it I?*" No, Peter, I foresee that you will deny that you know Me. That you will even swear that you do not. That you will even do this several times; but no, it is not you who will betray Me.

"*Lord, is it I?*" No, Thomas. You will run away for fear at my death, though you said you would die with Me. You will not believe My word that I am risen, and that I am your Lord, until you put your hand in the prints of the nails; but no, it is not you who will betray Me.

"*Lord, is it I?*" No, John. You shall be beside Me at the Cross. I mean that you shall have the charge of my mother; oh, no, I do not mean you!

"*Lord, is it I?*" Thou hast said it, Judas. I made you an Apostle, a pillar of my Church. I called you out of the world, and took you to my bosom, as a dear friend. You have gone in and out, and eaten and drunk with Me. Nay, you have just received My Body and Blood, and all the while you hold the thirty pieces of silver for which you have betrayed Me.

Now, then, I think I hear you say to me: Father, have I then done this horrible thing? *Is it I? Is it I?* No, my good man. You have enjoyed for years your ill-got gains, but your health has gone now. Declining years have come upon you, and you are poor; you can never restore them again. Your communions are not unworthy for this. But as for you, young man, why have you presumed to come to the altar? Where are those thirty pieces of silver for which you sold your soul? You promised in confession that you would restore them, but why? that you might get your Easter Communion. In your heart you said, Perhaps I will, some day, and all the while, you knew that no absolution is valid without the will to restore, or actual restitution when one is able; and you *were* able.

Father, is it I? No, poor fellow. You forgot to mention in your last confession, a very grievous sin, and only remembered it just after you had left the altar. Do not be troubled. You tried your best to examine your conscience, but this escaped your memory.

It was forgiven with the rest. But what have you to say for yourself, O drunkard? You did not leave out one of your many nights of debauch; but what of that solemn promise to keep from liquor for so long a time, which you have already so often broken, as you had no intention of keeping it? You have drunk in damnation with your liquor, and deeper damnation with your communion.

Father, is it I? No, poor girl. You should have known better than to have trusted yourself to a deceiver with his jewels and wine; but you have done penance. Your sobs in the confessional have spoken for you. Your communion, though so soon after your confession, was good. But what have you to say for yourself, O adulterer, and adulteress? You, O adulterer; you found a home where there were smiles, and fondness, and peace; and what have you done? You have made it a home of jealousy and strife. You have put estrangement between two hearts whom God joined together, and said, "let no man put asunder." You have robbed a fellow man of one of his most sacred rights given him in the face of the Church. And you, O adulteress, why have you come here? Our Lord said to Judas, "*Friend, why hast thou come? dost thou betray the Son of Man with a kiss?*" You knelt here at the altar-rail, and as the Priest said to you, "The Body of our Lord Jesus Christ preserve thy soul unto everlasting life," you put up your lips, and said, like Judas, 'Hail Master! and you kissed our Lord. Oh! where was the Angel of the Blessed Sacrament then? An Angel was placed at the gate of Eden with a flaming sword to keep guard over the Tree of Life. Oh! where, I ask, was the Angel of the Blessed Sacrament? Where was His guardian who said of Himself, "*I am the bread that cometh down from Heaven, of which whosoever eateth, he shall live forever!*" Preserve thy soul unto everlasting life, indeed! It has prepared you for the everlasting burnings; for the flames that shall never be quenched. You went to confession, you say! Yes, I know you did, and you concealed your sins of shame. You have added to these one of sacrilege. And you, O slanderer, who have robbed your neighbor of his character, by your lies and calumnies which you have never told in confession, or if you have, which you never intend to repair at the price of your own dishonor! You have been drinking in your own judgment with the Blood of Jesus. Jesus, judgment! Jesus, damnation! Why St. Bernard said, the very name of Jesus "was music in his ear, honey in his mouth, and joy to his heart." Jesus, damnation! Why St. Gabriel said *"He shall be called Jesus, for He shall save His people from their sins."* O cruel perversion of sin! to turn sweetness into bitterness! But what does God say of such as these? *"When you stretch forth your hands, I will turn away My eyes from you; and when you multiply prayer, I will not hear; for your hands are full of blood."**

Let me tell you a fact that a Jesuit told to one of our Fathers. A young man in the neighborhood where he lived, was heir to a large estate, which he was to receive at twenty-one years of age, on the condition that at that time he frequented the Sacraments. He turned out to be very wild and given up to sin. Near the end of his twentieth year, he was reminded of the danger of his losing the estate. Never fear, said he, I'll easily manage that, and

* Isaias i., 15.

at once he began to lead outwardly a very correct life. He was now seen at Mass. He kept out of society, and public places of amusement. Within a short time before his birthday, he went to confession; and the morning came, when he was seen to go up to the altar-rail for communion. The Priest placed the Blessed Sacrament on his tongue, and had turned back to the altar, when he heard a frightful shriek, and the words "My tongue! my tongue! it has burned my tongue!" When the Priest returned to him, he said, " Oh Father, forgive me, my confession was bad, I had been in the secret commission of mortal sins which I purposely concealed. I had no wish to forsake them, but only to secure my property; oh Father, I repent, absolve me before I die!" The Priest took the Blessed Sacrament from his tongue, and with much difficulty consoled him with the promise of pardon. He made a good communion soon after, and was put in possession of his estate, which he sold, and gave to the poor, and in penance for his sins, doomed his false tongue thenceforward to perpetual silence.

Tremble, then, dear brethren, at the thought

of so grievous a sin. For such as are guilty of it, there is but one thing to be done. Come back to God with sorrow, now in this time of penance, for, "*thus saith the Lord; if your sins be as scarlet they shall be made as white as snow; and if they be red as crimson they shall be as white as wool.*"* Confess your sacrilegious communions. Go and repair the scandal you have given. Restore the goods you have stolen. Abandon the companions of your guilt. Do this, and there will be joy before the Angels of God, and with the Priests to whom you may confide your conscience. If, in spite of all I have said, you live on with the guilt of an unworthy communion, eternal woe will be your portion; from which may God in His mercy deliver you, and all of us. AMEN.

* Isaias i., 13.

SERMON III.

CHRIST'S RESURRECTION THE FOUNDATION OF OUR FAITH.

"And when the Sabbath was past, Mary Magdalene and Mary the mother of James, and Salome, brought sweet spices."—Mark xvi., 1.

(From the Gospel for Easter Sunday.)

On this day, the bosom of the whole Church swells with exultation. After the penance of Lent, after the mourning of Holy Week, the countless disciples of the crucified and risen Saviour, take up and echo through the whole earth the joyful cry—Christ is risen! He is risen indeed. For this is the day on which Jesus Christ, bursting the bonds of the sepulchre, triumphed over death. This is the day which, more than any other, enlivens our faith, strengthens our hope of eternal salvation, and causes our hearts to bound with spiritual joy. Even the coldest and most indifferent Christian feels his bosom warm with some faint sentiment, at least, of devotion on this day, and remembers with pride that he bears the name and professes the faith of Jesus Christ. This is right and proper. For all the doctrines of our religion are centred in the resurrection. All our hopes are based upon it. The Resurrection is the grand Fact of Christianity. It is the proof of the Divinity of Jesus Christ; it is the seal of God which makes the documents of our faith authentic; it is the cause and the pledge of our final resurrection and eternal happiness. This accounts for the joy which swells every true Christian bosom, on this day. For, my dear brethren—and I beg you to note it well—the source of our hope and of our joy is in our faith. It is the certainty of faith which banishes all doubt, wavering, hesitation and gloom from the heart of a sincere and fervent Catholic. The faith of the Resurrection must be firmly planted in our minds, if we would have the hope of the Resurrection, and the joy which springs from this

3*

hope, bright and glowing in our hearts. Let me therefore ask your attention this morning, while I endeavor to show you what a firm and and immovable foundation we have for our faith, in the resurrection of Jesus Christ. And in doing so, I will endeavor to establish these three points:

First.—That Jesus Christ appealed to his future resurrection, while he was yet alive, as the proof of his Divinity.

Second.—That He actually raised himself from the dead, as he had predicted, and,

Third.—That the Resurrection of Christ proves his Deity, and with it, the entire Catholic faith.

May the grace of the risen Saviour increase our faith, through the intercession of Mary, whose faith never wavered for an instant, even beneath the Cross of her Son!

I.

Jesus Christ asserted frequently and clearly to the Jews, that he was God, and required them to believe him. So his disciples understood him, who believed; so the Jews understood him, who did not believe, but accused him of blasphemy and condemned him to death. The great sign, the miracle, the proof, to which he appealed to justify this declaration, was his resurrection on the third day after his death. He declared himself to be the proper and only begotten Son of God. He that does not believe this, he says, "*is already judged, because he believeth not in the Name of the only-begotten Son of God.*"* This title of only-begotten which he gives himself, shows that he does not merely claim to be a child of God by grace and adoption, but by nature. This nature he declares positively is not his human nature, but distinct from it, that it came from heaven, and was in heaven as well as on earth. "*No man hath ascended into heaven, but he that descended from heaven, the Son of Man who is in heaven.*"† He confesses that he is man; but asserts that he is more than man, that he came from heaven. He asserts also that this superior nature which is joined with his humanity is eternal. "*Before Abraham was—I am.*"‡ Not I was; but *I am*, the word by which God made known his eternity to Moses. And finally he declares that this super-

* John iii., 17. † John iii., 13. ‡ John viii., 58.

human and eternal nature is identical with that of his Father, is the Divine nature itself. "*I and my Father are one.*"* His disciples who believed in him, understood him to teach his divinity. "*My Lord and my God,*"† was the expression of the faith of Thomas. "*The Word was God,*"‡ that of John.

So the Jews understood him, who did not believe. "*The Jews answered him: for a good work we stone thee not, but for blasphemy, and because that thou, being a man,* MAKEST THYSELF GOD!"§ The Jews understood then perfectly well, that in calling himself the true, proper, and only Son of God, the Christ and Saviour of the world; and in working miracles, forgiving sins, and preaching salvation, in his own name, and by his own authority, and not as a mere prophet—he asserted his own true and proper divinity, and made himself God.

In support of this claim, Jesus Christ repeatedly appealed to his resurrection. He foretold his death; and declared that he would show himself to be the true Son of God the Father,

---

* John x., 38.   ‡ John i.
† John xx., 28.   § John x., 33.

having the same divine nature and the same divine power with him; by raising himself from the dead on the third day. "*The Son of Man shall be in the heart of the earth, three days and three nights.*"* This was said to the Scribes and Pharisees who wished him to give them a sign which should prove him to be the true Christ. When he drove out the men who were trafficking in the courts of the Temple, the Jews said to him: "*What sign dost thou show unto us, seeing thou dost these things? Jesus answered and said unto them: Destroy this temple, and in three days I will raise it up. But he spoke of the temple of his body.*"† It is remarkable that he does not declare that he will be raised to life by his Father, but by himself. "*I lay down my life that I may take it again. No man taketh it away from me, but I lay it down of myself, and I have power to lay it down; and I have power to take it up again.*"‡ These are only samples of the frequent and public declarations made by our Lord to the same effect. And it was so well known among the Jews that he had staked his entire cause on his res-

* Matt. xii., 40.   † John ii., 18.   ‡ John x., 17.

urrection, that they came to Pilate, immediately after his crucifixion, and said to him: "*Sir, we have remembered that that seducer said, while he was yet alive: After three days I will rise again. Command therefore the sepulchre to be guarded until the third day.*"*

Here, then, is the grand test of the truth of Christ's doctrine—the grand sign of his divinity; the public challenge which he gives to all his enemies. We have it on the testimony of the most desperate haters of his name and doctrine; the very men who nailed him to the Cross. They were resolved to prove his prediction false, to show that he could not, and would not, rise again, and thus to manifest him to the world as a seducer. At the sepulchre of Jesus Christ, then, is the trial of strength between them. The dead body of Jesus is on one side; the Jewish rulers, the Roman governor, and a strong watch of soldiers on the other. And Jesus Christ overcame; he actually did rise, as he had foretold: "*resurrexit sicut dixit;*" and all their precautions only served to furnish so many brilliant testimonies to the fact, that he had fulfilled his word.

* Matt. xxvii., 63.

II.

Picture to yourselves, if you can, the scenes of those three memorable days! The Sun of Justice, the Light of the World, has gone down in darkness. Jesus Christ is dead; he is buried, and a great stone is rolled to the door of the sepulchre. The disciples are scattered here and there, buried in the most profound and bitter disappointment, consternation and grief. The multitudes have fled hastily from Mount Calvary, some beating their breasts with contrition, some blaspheming, but all in terror. The heavens are overclouded and black, the thunder moans, and an earthquake shakes the earth. The frightened inhabitants of Jerusalem, as they return to their homes, are met in the streets by the pale corpses of the dead, who have left their graves, and are wandering about among the living. In the temple, those wicked and unworthy priests are startled at the sudden tearing, by an invisible hand, of the thick and heavy veil which hangs before the Holy of Holies. An ominous stillness sinks over the city of Jerusalem after that dreadful, tragical day. It is the eve of the greatest Sabbath of the year. The Sabbath morning dawns once more; all is apparently quiet, and God does not appear, to take sudden vengeance on his guilty people. Annas and Caiphas, and those other wicked priests who have sacrificed the Lamb of God, with their souls all black and turbid with remorse, but with a grim and diabolical exultation in the success of their horrid work, prepare themselves in splendid vestments for the sacrifices and the ceremonies of the day. The countless multitudes of Jews, gathered together from every part of the world to keep the Passover, crowd the vast courts of the temple. The disciples remain shut up, in silence and in fear. The Roman soldiers guard the shut and sealed sepulchre of Jesus. The day passes and the night, and nothing occurs. The first streaks of the dawn begin to appear in the sky on Sunday morning. The disciples have forgotten the promise of their Master to rise on the third day, and have lost heart entirely. Mary Magdalene, and the other pious women, have planned to steal out early to visit his tomb, and to bring their spices, and perfumes, and fresh flowers, to cast upon his dead body. They set forth together; while still in the distance, they are frightened by the sight of torches and armed men in the garden. They have not courage to go on; and they remember that a great stone is at the door of the sepulchre, which will hinder their entrance. Only the courageous and loving Mary Magdalene has the hardihood to press forward at all risks, leaving the others hovering about in the neighborhood of the garden. As she approaches the sepulchre, she sees the stone rolled away to one side; she pays no attention to the soldiers who are lying on the ground, apparently stunned and insensible, but goes in, and the body of Jesus Christ is not there; his graveclothes are lying in the spot where his body was placed, and an angel is watching the empty sepulchre. Bewildered and surprised, and occupied only with the thought that the body is gone, she runs hastily back to the place where John and other apostles are staying, tells them in breathless haste what she has seen, and without waiting for a reply, returns as speedily as possible to the sepulchre. Meanwhile, during Magdalene's absence, the other women observing that the soldiers have left the gar-

den, come also to the sepulchre, see the stone rolled away, go in, and find two angels sitting, one at the head, the other at the foot of the place where Christ was laid. The angels tell them that Christ is risen, and bid them go announce it to his disciples, and direct them to meet him in Galilee, as he had commanded them before his death. They now leave the garden to return to the city, and Magdalene arrives once more, and while these things are happening **the sun** has risen, the sun of the first Easter Sunday, the type of the Risen Sun of Justice. Mary Magdalene goes into the sepulchre again, and **begins** to weep, still too much occupied with the thought that the body of Christ is gone, to reflect on any thing else. She sees the angels; but to the questions: "*Woman, why weepest thou? whom seekest thou?*" she answers distractedly, "*They have taken away my Lord, and I know not where they have laid him.*" She turns around, and sees the figure of a man, whom she takes to be the gardener, and asks him where they have taken the body of Jesus. The well-known voice exclaims: "Mary!" She suddenly recognizes the Lord, and utters a cry of joy: "Oh, my Master!" She tries to clasp him by the feet, but he forbids her, and bids her go, announce his resurrection to the disciples. She sets off immediately, and in a few moments Peter and John arrive, visit the sepulchre, and see that the body is not there. They also return to the city. Immediately after his interview with Mary Magdalene, the Lord appears also to her companions, while they are returning to their homes. He was also seen by Peter some time during the day. Toward evening he joins two of the disciples, who were going to Emmaus, a small village near Jerusalem, and explains to them the prophecies of the Scripture concerning himself, but is not recognized by them, until he blesses bread and gives it to them, and then disappears from view. So the day passes. First one arrives at the cœnaculum, and relates his story, then another, then others; the day passes in comparing these different accounts, in conversing together, in expectation of what is going to happen. When night draws on, the apostles and disciples are gathered together for prayer; the two from Emmaus come in just then, and relate their interview with the Lord, when suddenly he appears among them, and says: "*Peace be unto you.*" So passes this day. The four Evangelists give no regular and methodical account of it. All these occurrences are related by some one or more of them; and I have **strung** them together in an order in which they might have happened, and which reconciles all the accounts with each other.

Such is the narrative of the Gospel. Is it true? Did these things really happen? In regard to one fact, Christians, Jews and Romans were agreed. The body of Jesus Christ **was** removed **from** a closed and sealed tomb, guarded by Roman soldiers, by early dawn on the morning of Easter Sunday. It was removed either by Divine power, or by human inge**nuity.** The rulers of the Jews circulated the report, which they have repeated to this day, **that** his disciples came and stole him away, while the guard was sleeping. "What!" exclaims St. Augustine, "you will prove your cause by sleeping witnesses?" If they were asleep, they knew nothing of the way by which the body disappeared. And if they were **awake** to see the disciples steal it, why did they not kill **them on** the spot. The guard were sleeping! A guard of Roman soldiers. Who can believe that? For a Roman soldier to sleep at his post was an extraordinary and most disgraceful thing, and here we have a whole band of them, with an officer at their head— sleeping. The punishment was death. In this case especially, no mercy could have been expected, where both Roman and Jewish rulers were so deeply interested in putting an end to the religion of Christ. How did they dare confess their sleeping, unless they were in connivance with the authorities, and bribed to repeat this story. Why was no trial held? Why were not these soldiers examined before a tribunal? Why was no search made for the body of Jesus, and for his disciples? Why is the whole matter hushed up by common consent between Pilate and Caiphas? There is only one possible supposition. And that is: that the soldiers saw the resurrection of the Lord—that they related it to their rulers, and that by bribes and threats their testimony was suppressed. I will not pause to accumulate arguments. I will not speak of the impossibility that Jesus Christ should be able to predict that his disciples would attempt such an incredible task as the removal of his body, and succeed in it. I will not speak of their timidity, **and their** perfect want of all plan of action, all means of carrying **out any** project whatever; of their complete perplexity and helplessness; **and of** the utter madness of sacrificing all their **worldly goods and their lives,** to carry out a manifest imposture. These things are so plain, that reasoning only seems to weaken the effect **with** which they strike conviction to the mind at the first statement.

I return to this simple fact, that the tale circulated by the soldiers, in common with Pilate and the Jewish rulers, is a complete and irresistible proof of the Resurrection. And there are evidences in abundance that it was so regarded at the time, that this incredible tale was only believed by the most stupid and besotted portion of the populace, and by those who knew nothing of the matter, except what **they heard** by vague rumors. We have the testimony of Tertullian that even Pilate was convinced of the truth of the resurrection, "Ea omnia super Christo Pilatus, et ipse pro conscientia sua jam Christianus, Tiberio renuntiavit."*

* Apol., c. 21.

Josephus, the Jewish historian, says of Christ, that "he appeared to them alive again, the third day, as the divine prophets had foretold."* Justin Martyr, a most learned Jew, and an eminent philosopher of the second century, who became a Christian, does not fear to assert boldly to the Jews: "You know that Jesus was risen from the dead and ascended into heaven, as the prophecies did foretell was to happen."† The fact of the Resurrection of Jesus Christ was so evident, that it paralyzed for a time the efforts of the Jewish rulers to suppress his doctrine. And months elapsed, during which this doctrine made the most astonishing progress, before they dared to put a disciple of Christ to death. It was the manifest fact of the resurrection which caused the sudden and continuous growth and propagation of the Christian Church. Jesus Christ was far more powerful after his death than during his life. Not only did several thousand of the most sincere and pious among the Jews of Jerusalem and Judea, and of the strangers who had come to celebrate the Passover, embrace Christianity, but "*a great multitude of*

* Antiq., Lib. xviii., c. 3. † Dial. cum. Tryph., p. 230.

the priests also were obedient to the faith."* Nicodemus, one of the most distinguished Doctors of the Law, and Joseph of Arimathea, a wealthy and powerful Jew, and a member of the grand council, who had previously been timid, and had abstained from attaching themselves openly to Christ, came out now publicly and announced themselves Christians. The centurion, or Roman officer, who commanded the soldiers by whom Christ was crucified, with the soldier who pierced the side of our Lord, and several other soldiers, were converted. The tremendous impression made by the resurrection of Christ on the whole Jewish nation, was the cause which gave the impetus to this movement. And it was the resurrection to which the apostles constantly appealed in proof of the divine character of Jesus Christ, and the truth of his doctrine.

III.

Thus did Jesus Christ, by raising himself from the dead, as he had foretold, redeem his pledge, and prove himself to be God. There-

* Acts i.

fore the Scripture frequently speaks as if Jesus Christ were made the Son of God by his resurrection. "He was," says St. Paul, "*predestinated the Son of God in power, by the resurrection from the dead.*"* That is, as St. Ambrose explains it—"He, whose deity was concealed in the incarnation, was predestinated to declare and manifest himself as the Son of God by his resurrection." During his life, he declared himself to be God, and promised to raise himself from the dead on the third day after his death, as a proof of his divinity. He did rise from the dead; and the resurrection is thus the grand proof of the central doctrine of the Catholic faith, the divinity of Christ, and not only of that, but also of every other doctrine connected with it and springing from it—of the Catholic faith complete and entire. It proves not merely the divinity of Christ, but the divinity of his words and of his acts. His words are words of divine truth; his acts are acts of divine power. The same Jesus who raised himself from the dead, said, "*This is my body—This is my Blood;*" and if we believe that he is truly God, we must be-

* Romans i. 4.

lieve that the Holy Eucharist is indeed his flesh and blood. The same Jesus who proved his divine power by raising himself from the dead, transferred and delegated his power to St. Peter and his successors, when he said—"*Thou art Peter, and on this Rock I will build my Church, and the gates of hell shall not prevail against it, and I will give to thee the keys of the kingdom of heaven; whatever thou shalt bind on earth shall be bound in heaven, and whatever thou shalt loose on earth shall be loosed in heaven.*" It is in the Catholic Church that the testimony to the resurrection, commenced by the first apostles, is continued and passed down from age to age, by the unbroken succession of popes and bishops. The apostles were the witnesses of the resurrection. When the new apostle was to be appointed in the place of Judas, St. Peter said—"*One of these must be made a witness with us of his resurrection.*"* The Catholic priesthood, as it were, joining hands with each other, run back in an unbroken line to the first fathers and founders of their glorious order, who saw the risen Saviour, and clasped the hands

* Acts i., 22.

nailed to the cross. Down this line has passed the uninterrupted, unbroken testimony to the resurrection. This day itself, the festival, Easter, is a grand monument of the resurrection. Every year, from this day back to the day on which Christ rose from the dead, the whole Christian Church has celebrated the resurrection of Christ on Easter Sunday. Thus we all join hands with our predecessors in past ages, until the long chain terminates in the little church of the disciples, gathered together in the cœnaculum, to whom Christ appeared and said — "Peace be to you." And as we celebrate these joyous festivities, which carry us back to the very days of our Lord and his apostles, an electric shock of faith startles and reanimates our souls. Yes; this is the day of faith. It is the special festival of faith. The resurrection confirmed and renewed the wavering, sinking faith of the disciples. "*The Lord has risen indeed, and has appeared unto Simon.*" These words show how those fainting and almost despairing hearts revived on that day. Oh! wretched and miserable men, such as Pilate and Caiphas, and the besotted multitude, who did not, would not believe—or at least would not act on their convictions, and confess the truth! Equally unhappy are those now, who have no faith; who do not believe in the Son of God; who do not await the resurrection of the dead; who believe in nothing, but pass their lives in miserable and endless doubting and unbelief.

Equally unhappy are those who, though enlightened once in baptism, and brought up from childhood in the Catholic faith, are weak, wavering and hesitating in their faith; who neither believe or disbelieve; who dare not renounce their religion, and yet will not adhere to it firmly and profess it openly; but hang, as it were, in the outskirts of faith, and around the courts of the temple of Divine Truth.

Equally unhappy are those who, believing firmly, deny their faith by their acts, and disobey the Lord whom they acknowledge to be their true God and their final Judge; who, on the day when Christ is risen from the dead, lie buried in the grave of mortal sin; who have no part in his life and grace, and have not received his Paschal sacraments.

But blessed are they who believe; whose

hearts are full of faith, and whose works correspond with that faith;—into whose bosoms the Paschal joy has entered by the devout reception of the Sacraments of Penance and the Eucharist, and who can look forward with hope to the day of the general resurrection from the dead. For all such good Christians, this is the brightest, the happiest, the most glorious day of the whole year. All things sympathize with the joy of the risen Saviour. The earth breaks the icy bonds of winter, and starting from the state of lifelessness, awakes to new life and growth and freshness. The spring begins to appear, and the signs of approaching warmth and of the time of buds and blossoms and green foliage show themselves. The Church puts on her festal attire and sends up her joyous hymns, and solemnizes her splendid ceremonies. The faithful everywhere, leave their sins, do penance for their misdeeds, weep at the foot of the cross, reconcile themselves with God, and come with purified hearts to partake of the Paschal Lamb—the flesh and blood of the Divine Jesus, in the blessed Sacrament of the altar. And while we go back in our thoughts to that day on which

Christ arose, the first-begotten from the dead, all these external signs and ceremonies point also forward to that last Easter Sunday—that day of the resurrection of all mankind. The change and renovation of the earth in the season of spring, and the resurrection of souls by the Paschal sacraments, and the solemn celebration of Christ's resurrection, these are all types of that glorious morning when the redeemed human race shall start from its tomb; when the old things shall pass away, and all things, the heaven and the earth, and all things that are in them, shall be made anew. When the obscurity of faith shall give place to the light of glory, and the hope of salvation shall be changed into the beatific vision of God.

SERMON IV.

GIVING TESTIMONY.

"You shall give testimony of me."—John xv., 27.

(From the Gospel for the 6th Sunday after Pent.)

THESE words were spoken by our Lord to his disciples, before his departure from this world. He had chosen them from the beginning, and imparted to them a full knowledge of the truth, that they might bear testimony to it. "*All things whatsoever I have heard from my Father I have made known to you.*"—"*I have chosen you, and have appointed you, that you should go, and should bring forth fruit, and your fruit should remain.*"* The disciples did give testimony. They labored in season and out of season in spreading the truths which

* John xv., 15, 16.

they had learned from the lips of our Saviour. "*Their sound went over all the earth, and their words unto the ends of the world.*"* Their testimony was not only in sound and words: their lives testified to the truth which they preached. They suffered persecution, poverty, imprisonment, and sealed their testimony to the truth with their blood, by willingly laying down their lives for it. These disciples were true to Christ. Their testimony was faithful, loyal, heroic. We, too, are disciples of Christ, and have our testimony to give; and I propose to show in the first place, what are our obligations to give this testimony of Christ; and in the second place, who are those who fail in in their obligations to give this testimony.

What are our obligations to give testimony of Christ? There are many Christians who seem to think that they are at liberty to choose what course of life they please, that they can live as they like; that whether they attend to their religious duties or neglect them, whether they are patterns of Christian virtue or scandals to their faith, is nobody's business. This opinion is false, most false, because all Chris-

* Rom. x., 18.

tians are under a lasting obligation to Christ to lead a Christian life.

Christ is our Lord and Master, and as such has a complete right of control over all our actions. There can be no dispute about this. "*You call me Master and Lord,*" says he; "*You say well, for so I am.*"* Christ is not only our Master and Lord, but also our Creator, "*for by Him all things were made that are made.*" His dominion over us is therefore absolute and supreme. In His presence we are simply subjects, and have only duties to fulfil.

Christ as Man has the full right of purchase over us. He can claim of us all our actions, for he redeemed us from the captivity and slavery of sin. "*Knowing that you were not redeemed,*" says the Apostle Peter to the faithful, "*with corruptible gold or silver from your vain conversation of the tradition of your fathers; but with the precious blood of Christ.*"† Can any one who listens to these words be so destitute of intelligence and faith as to entertain the idea, for a moment, that God created us and became man and died for

---

* 1 John xiii., 13.   † 1 Peter i., 18. 19.

4*

us, only to leave us at liberty to live as we please, and to sin as much and as often as we like? No; says the Apostle Paul, "*Christ died for all.*" And why? Listen, faithless Christian: "*That they also who live may not live to themselves, but to Him who died for them, and rose again.*"* What is it to live to Christ? To live to Christ is, to live to please Him; it is to follow in His footsteps and copy in our lives His virtues. This is made clear from what the same Apostle says in another place, on the same subject: "*Our Saviour, Jesus Christ, gave Himself for us, that He might redeem us from all iniquity, and purify unto Himself a people, acceptable, pursuing good works.*"† A Christian, then, is one who lives to Christ by keeping free from all iniquity and pursuing good works. This is the testimony that Christ requires of us, and which we are bound to give by every sacred obligation which binds us to Him as our Creator and Redeemer.

Another reason why we are under obligation to give testimony of Christ by leading an exemplary life, is that Christ came into the

* 1 Cor. v., 15.   † 2 Titus ii., 14.

world not only to be our Redeemer, but also our Model. Hear him: "*You call me Master and Lord, and you say well, for so I am, ... and if I, then, being your Lord and Master have given you an example, as I have done to you, so you do also.*"* For is there any one so uninstructed as not to know that it was wholly unnecessary for Jesus Christ to practise on his own account, humiliations, poverty, obedience, self-denial, meekness, and embrace the sufferings and bitter death of the cross. He practised these virtues in order to induce us to practise them, for these were due to us as punishment for our sins, and necessary for us as preservatives against our vices. God became man to teach men by example how they ought to live. "*Christ suffered for us,*" says the apostle St. Peter, "*leaving you an example, that you should follow his steps.*"† He then is false and faithless to his obligations, who claims the name of a Christian, and does not follow in Christ's footsteps. No Christian, then, has the right to live as he likes, but is bound to live as Christ likes.

The Holy Church too, has a right to exact

---

* St. John xiii., 13, 14, 15.   † 1 Peter ii., 21.

from us the obligation to lead an exemplary life. For as in a flock of pigeons, on seeing one fly all the others follow, so it is in the society of the Church, the good example of one member encourages and edifies the whole body. That you may understand the watchfulness and jealousy of our Lord over his flock, listen to his own language: "*He that shall scandalize one of these little ones that believe in me, it were better that a mill-stone were hanged about his neck, and that he were drowned in the depths of the sea. . . . Woe to that man by whom scandal cometh.*"* The Church has not only the right to claim from us to follow in Christ's footsteps for the sake of believers, but also for the unbeliever. According to the words of Christ: "*Let your light so shine before men that they may see your good works, and glorify your Father in heaven.*"† It is more by the testimony of a good example than by miracles, that unbelievers are brought to the light of truth. This is illustrated by the example of the martyr St. Lucien. It is related of him by Surius, that he led many unbelievers to the knowledge of the truth

---

* Matt. xviii., 6, 7. † Matt. v., 16.

and to embrace the Catholic faith, by the modesty of his life and his exemplary conduct. So powerful was the influence of his example, that the Emperor Maximilian, when seated upon his throne and about to condemn him to death, commanded that he should be kept out of his view, behind a veil, lest even the mere sight of the saint should change him into a Christian. Is it not then with good reason St. John Chrysostom says: "There would be no heathens were we such Christians as we ought to be.... Paul was but a man, yet how many did he draw after him! If we were all such as he, how many worlds might we have drawn to us!"* How was it St. Paul attracted so many to Christ? He tells us himself, in these words: "*Give no offence to the Jews, nor to the gentiles, nor to the church of God; as I also please all men in all things, not seeking that which is profitable to myself, but to many; that they may be saved.*"†

It is clear, then, beyond all dispute, that every one who claims the name of a Christian is bound by a lasting and sacred obligation to give testimony to Christ by following in his footsteps,

* 1 Tim. Hom, x. † 1 Cor. x.. 31, 32.

and consequently those who fail are guilty of robbing their Lord and Master of his rights, and are no true Catholics, but traitors to the faith.

Who are they who fail to give this testimony of Christ? I will tell you.

You will find many who were born of Catholic parents, were baptized in the faith when young, and yet never acknowledging the faith of their fathers, and of their baptism. They are not open apostates, they neither attack their faith, nor defend it when attacked. You might know them for years and not dream that they were Catholics. It is hard to tell what they really are. They are not Protestants, nor Jews, nor Turks, for these have religious convictions, and do not deny them, but the men I speak of either have no religious convictions, or want the manliness to acknowledge them. They do not like to be known as Catholics, and yet they identify themselves publicly with free-masons, odd-fellows, and similar secret societies.

Another class consists of those who confess themselves Catholics, but never, or very rarely, enter the Church. They take offence at the slightest irregularity, whether it be in the priesthood, or the preaching, or in the manner of conducting public worship; and under some such pretext they excuse their grievous neglect of worship, and their profound indifference to all the sacred duties of religion. These claim the name of Catholic, and their conduct is that of an infidel.

A third class is composed of those who now and then on occasion of a jubilee or a mission, or some similar event, come to Church, and perhaps receive the holy sacraments. Their religion is like a fire in the straw, it soon dies out. Talk to these men of their business, and they will tell you that a man who does not watch and pay constant attention to it, will soon find himself bankrupt. Speak to them of the affairs of the nation, and they will tell you that the country is going to ruin, because its citizens neglect to attend political meetings and fail to approach the polls at election times. On business, or politics, on almost every thing but their religion, they reason correctly, and act like sensible men; on their duties to God and the affairs of their soul they appear to be as destitute of reason as they are of loyalty.

Money is their God, and their religion is politics.

The fourth class is made up of the rank and file of sinners—cursers, drunkards, and the army of grog-shop keepers. These latter, under the pretext of making a living, spread more misery, wretchedness, and crime among our people, than all the plagues of Egypt brought upon the inhabitants of that land. The source of nine-tenths of the scandal to our holy religion is in the grog-shops; and to make the scandal of their vile and unlawful traffic more conspicuous, they congregate by preference in the neighborhood of a Church, justifying the well-known proverb:

> "Where God erects a house of prayer,
> Satan must have a chapel there."

The grog-shop keepers are the worst enemies of our holy religion in this country, for they not only occasion the destruction of a vast number of Catholics, but by the disgust which their bad example creates, they offer the greatest hindrances to the conversion of non-catholics.

These are some out of the great number of those who fail to give testimony of Christ; for we have not the time to enumerate all. Now, what is very strange, and yet characteristic of all these, they appear to live as though they were unconscious of their obligations, and of the guilt which they incur. They seem to think that if they are allowed to assume the name of a Christian or Catholic, they are safe. Well then, asks one, why not exclude them from the Church altogether, so that the whole world can see what they are? This is the way we do away with unprofitable subjects in other institutions. Take, for example, a railroad corporation. Sometimes a company of this kind starts with great prospects. The number who travel on the road is prodigious. The stockholders congratulate themselves on a heavy dividend; when to their wonder, on reckoning up their accounts, they find the company running fast into bankruptcy. Investigations are made, and it is discovered that a large number of the passengers have been paying no fare, riding as "dead-heads." These being struck off, the corporation begins to prosper again. Not so with the holy Church. She is in this respect unlike all other institutions. She is likened by her Founder to a field of wheat, in which the enemy had sown cockle. And when one of the servants said to the master: "*Wilt thou that we go to gather it up? and he said, no; lest while you gather up the cockle, you root up the wheat also together with it. Let both grow until the harvest; and in the time of harvest, I will say to the reapers, gather up first the cockle, and bind it into bundles to burn; but gather the wheat into my barn.*"*

The time to cut off the faithless children, the "dead-heads" of the Church, is not now, but "in the harvest time," the day of general reckoning, when our Lord shall appear in power and majesty to judge the world. Then he will say to these: "I am your Lord and Master, why have you not obeyed me?" He will show them his wounds, and say: "Behold the price I paid to redeem you from sin! What right had you to refuse my service? I came upon earth to give an example that you might follow my steps, and you turned your back upon me! You were a scandal to the Church, and a stumbling-block in the way of others. You refused to give testimony to my mercy, now you shall give testimony to my sovereign justice. Gather up this cockle, these faithless,

* Matt. xiii., 28, etc.

false, treacherous disciples," he will say to his servants, "and let their portion be in the pool which burns with fire and brimstone."*

Could but our voice reach the ears, and our entreaties penetrate the hearts of these guilty Catholics, we would lift it up and cry out to them: Do penance speedily! Repair by a good example the evil which your bad example has caused to your neighbor. Strive to gain more souls to Christ than your wicked life has lost to him heretofore. Let your good works shine out the more, so that like the servant of the eleventh hour, you may obtain the full wages of eternal life.

As for you, dearest brethren, who have manfully withstood until now all temptations to be disloyal to your faith, whose lives, full of good works, have borne noble testimony to Christ, lift up your eyes and hearts to heaven at this season of our Lord's ascension. "*I go,*" he says, "*to prepare a place for you. I will come again, and will take you to myself; that where I am, you may be also.*"†

* John xxi., 8. Apoc.   † John xiv., 2, 3.

SERMON V.

SPIRITUAL DEATH.

"Behold! a dead man was carried out."—St. Luke vii., 12.

(From the Gospel of the 15th Sunday after Pent.)

What a touching occasion was this, in which our Blessed Lord was pleased to manifest his power, and perform one of his many acts of infinite mercy; an act, which like all his miracles, was not only full of loving-kindness to those for whom it was performed, but also replete with spiritual instruction for all.

A widow is bereaved of her only consolation, a son, in whom were centred all her hopes, in whose happiness all her own was bound up; the pride of her eyes, her joy in adversity, and the sunshine to her poor heart in the cloudy days of sorrow.

Perhaps, too, he was her only support; his the arm which labored for their daily bread, and she looked forward to the time when age and gray hairs should bring infirmity, and her enfeebled body tremble on the verge of the grave; then would he be the light to her dimmed eyes, and a guide to her tottering steps.

And now, alas! he is gone! Is the world all dead? Is it always night? Do the birds sing no more? Are the earth and sky all wrapped in a great, gloomy mantle of grief? Where is her heart, does it beat no more? Ah! so it is indeed to her.

How she watched him in the long hours of his racking pains, his burning fever. At times he did not know her; *her*, his own dear mother. Oh! how she prayed for him. Oftentimes, as he lay upon his dying bed unconscious, she would kneel down beside him, and take his thin wasted hand in hers, and lift up her streaming eyes to God, the Father of the fatherless, and pour forth her soul in an agony of supplication, beseeching Him to spare her only son, her life, her all.

In vain. That hand grows cold within her grasp; those eyes, which erewhile were so full of expression, have assumed a dull glassy unmeaning stare, there is one shuddering convulsion, the breathing ceases, his jaw drops, and she is a broken-hearted, childless widow. That body, once so cherished and tenderly cared for, must soon be removed far away out of sight, and now, amid the lamentations of a sympathizing multitude, they carry it to the grave. She feels her loss so keenly that the very carriers of the bier seem to her to be heartless and unfeeling. Thus the scene in the Gospel opens: "*Behold, a dead man is carried out.*" I know that poor widow. I have seen that dead man, her only son, the cherished idol of her heart, many a time. I know well those bearers, and they are assuredly most heartless and unfeeling. I have seen the Lord stop them on their way, as they carried him to the portals of death and hell.

Would you know who they are? Sinner! offspring of Holy Mother Church, part and parcel of her own life, who by sin hast lost the life of grace; it is thou! Behold thou art the dead man who is carried out. Contemplate thyself as in a mirror in this example from the Holy Gospel.

The Church has done for you all, aye, and more than this poor widow did, or could do, for her only son.

She has given you a noble birth in Jesus Christ. She nourished you, watched over, and cared for you, in your infancy. She flattered herself, poor mother, that you would do honor to her one day; she looked forward to the time when you would become her support. She was so bound up in you, that she often exclaimed with a truth, "Why do I live if it be not for my child?" Her very occupation, her unceasing labors were for you. How proud she was to see you increasing in grace with God and men, your manly soul strong in virtue; your conscience bright and fair to look upon as the face of an angel, thrilling her maternal heart with gladness, as she beheld reflected there the lineaments of the sacred countenance of her Divine Spouse.

Alas! that any thing so bright and beautiful should ever know decay or death!

Hear the sad story. Disease came. Sin entered into your soul, as does the insidious pestilence into the very marrow of the bones. And now the frightened mother looks with dismay upon your changed features. You are becoming emaciated, your soul, starving in sickness, is no longer cheerful with the love of God. Although so haggard and so woebegone, there is yet the hectic flush of the fever of passion. At times in the height of that fever your mind wanders: you do not know her, *her!* your own dear mother? So low has sin brought you, so far has sin abased you, that you have forgotten your noble descent and your glorious destiny. The crime of disobedience to the law of God has done its work, and that soul which once walked so proudly erect now lies completely prostrated.

Oh! how that Mother Church prays for you! With outstretched arms to heaven she implores the divine mercy. "*Spare, O Lord, spare thy people, and give not thine heritage to reproach.*" Leave me not alone without this only son of my heart, for whom Christ died! But you are in your agony now, and hear nothing. You are not moved to tears, as you would be, if you could but hear those agonizing prayers. You lie indifferent to all around, while the disease fastens upon your very vitals: one sin after another, one temptation given way to after another, until the life-blood of your soul has frozen in its channels: and before your weeping, inconsolable mother, the Church— before God, and in sight of His holy Angels and Saints, you are dead! dead!! dead!!!

Like the fruitless church of Sardis, in the Apocalypse: "*Thou hast a name that thou livest, but art dead.*"*

What are the signs, my brethren, by which you would pronounce a man dead? Surely, that he has no longer the use of any of his senses; that he can neither see, hear, taste, touch nor smell. If nothing remained to him but faint breathing, and a fluttering, feeble pulse, you would already weep for him as lost to you, and consider it only as the matter of a few moments to draw the sheet over his face, and prepare his shroud.

Now this is just the deplorable state of a man in mortal sin.

Let me illustrate this. If you saw a person walking upon a railroad track, and the train came thundering along directly in front of him, and yet he proceeded on his way, totally unmindful of your shouts and warnings of dan-

* Apoc. iii., 1.

ger, you would throw up your hands and exclaim: "Ah! God have mercy on him, poor man; he must be totally blind and deaf—he is as good as dead." And so he is in effect; for the train passes over him, and scatters his mangled body hither and thither. Of what use to him was his power of motion? He had the name of a living man, and is dead. So death is coming upon you, sinner, sudden and destructive. How many sermons have you not heard upon that awful subject? How many warnings have you not had in the deaths, ever unlooked for, alas! too often unprovided for, among your friends, acquaintances, and in the very bosom of your family. You hear not, you see not; no warning will turn you from your fatal track. You are as good as dead.

If you saw a young girl walking to the brink of one of those dreadful precipices formed by the lofty palisades on the North River, and, despite the cries of her friends, she continued her walk, gazing up at the sky, would you not say: "Ah! poor thing, she must be killed; she is as good as dead." Oh, young woman, you are walking upon the brink of a precipice, by your dangerous familiarities, your late hours, your improper company-keeping; and despite the cries of your father, your mother, the pleadings of your friends, and the warning voice of your confessor, your heedlessness in sin will destroy you, body and soul, and you must lose reputation, honor, salvation, eternity. Deaf to the voice of God, you are as good as dead.

Jesus daily prepares his divine banquet for you; but, alas! you have lost your spiritual taste for that heavenly food, and there is no life in you—you are dead; according to the words of the divine Saviour: "*Amen, Amen. I say unto you, Except ye eat the flesh of the Son of Man, and drink his blood, you shall not have life in you.*"*

The Lord strikes you with afflictions of various kinds: disease, loss of friends, misfortune in your business. He sends his angel of death to your very doors; but you are insensible to his chastisements: they affect you no more than if you were a statue of marble. Is not this to be indeed dead?

"*You have put on malediction as a vest-*

---
* St. John vi., 54.

ment, and it has entered like water into your veins, and as oil into your bones."* Yes; corruption has commenced; you have become offensive as a corpse, of bad odor, and scandalous to the Christian community. The finger is pointed at you, your bad life is everywhere spoken of, but you do not believe it; like a corpse, you are not sensible of the disgust you excite. As the sister of Lazarus said to the Lord: "*It is now four days since he died, and already he stinketh.*" Four days! Why, it is four months—four years—forty years, since *you* died—since you committed mortal sin, and continued in it, oh! unrepentant sinner; and you have become insupportable. You have reaped the blasting curse you sowed: "*For he that soweth in the flesh, of the flesh also shall reap corruption,*" the words of this day's Epistle.† Your dead soul is in the hands of the bearers, your companions in sin, your fellow cursers and blasphemers. The grog-shop keepers have got hold of you, and every step is a closer approach to the tomb, the gates of hell, the last home of fornicators, liars, and drunkards. How insensible you lie in their

* Psalms cviii., 18.   † Gal. vi., 8.

SPIRITUAL DEATH. 85

hands! The multitude may weep, in company with your poor mother, piercing cries and sobs which are heard throughout heaven and hell, but make no impression on your dull ears. No! there is no sound can wake you now, but the voice of Jesus Christ, or the last trump which will summon your guilty soul to judgment.

Will that voice of Jesus Christ be heard? I know not. Will the Lord be moved to pity toward his weeping Church? I know not. Will he touch the bier upon which you are stretched stark dead, and command those companions of yours in sin to stop? I know not. Will Jesus arrest the steps of that infamous woman, of those debased, pitiless, heartless, unfeeling dram-sellers? (Did I not say that the widow was right—that they are heartless and unfeeling?) I know not. What I do know is that, if Jesus is not moved to pity, if he does not strike fear into the heart of that young man or woman, your companion in sin, if the arm of the vengeance of Christ does not fall upon that grog-shop keeper,—no other sound will waken you, so dead in sin, but that one upon the Last Day, which rather than to hear, it were better for you to sleep in eternal oblivion.

"Ah! father," you say, "that's dreadful doctrine." Yes; and there is something more dreadful about it. It is true. What saith the Apostle? "*It is impossible for those who were once illuminated and have tasted the heavenly gift,* **and are fallen** *away,* **to be** *renewed again to penance, crucifying again to themselves the Son of God, and making him a mockery.*"* What **does this** mean but that, when one has fallen away into mortal sin, it is as impossible for him to do any thing toward the salvation of his soul, as it is for a dead man to raise himself to life. **Lay it** to heart—a most important truth—that Almighty God owes you nothing; is not bound, nor has he promised, to give you grace beyond a certain degree; while he has most emphatically warned the sinner that the time will come, and who knows—oh! dreadful thought—but that it has already arrived for you, when he will withdraw his countenance from you, and leave you to the fate you have chosen, and so justly merited. Every child has amused himself on the banks

* Heb. vi., 4.

of the river or brook, watching the eddies caused by the meeting of contrary currents, and observing how the brown leaves which have fallen from the trees into the stream are suddenly caught in the circling current and whirled about, approaching at each revolution nearer the centre of it. Now, we are told by travellers, that in the vast ocean there are powerful and dangerous eddies of this sort, called whirlpools; and that large ships, if allowed to sail within their influence, are drawn in, and carried round and round, no longer obedient to the sails or rudder, and at last are completely swallowed up in the yawning vortex of whirling waters.

Oh! unrepentant sinner: you are the brown leaf, fallen from the tree of life into the water of iniquity. You are the ship which has lost its compass, and strayed within reach of the dizzy whirlpool. God stood upon the calm open sea, and each time that you came around he warned you of your danger. He did more; he sent strong and sufficient breezes of his holy grace; if you had taken advantage of them in trimming the sails, and putting up the helm, you might have escaped. How many times did he not thus attempt your rescue: but you heeded him not. There was even something pleasant and intoxicating to be thus carried along in the powerful stream; and now you go faster and faster, nearer and nearer, until the yawning abyss opens upon your gaze, and you send forth a shriek for help, a cry of despair. But you are so dizzy that you cannot descry the form of God upon the sea. It is well; it would double your agony to see him now, for he has turned his back upon you; or worse, is mocking you, and laughs you to scorn. "*Because I called and you refused; I stretched out my hand, and there was none that regarded. You have despised all my counsel, and have neglected my reprehensions. I also will laugh in your destruction, and will mock when your fear cometh. When sudden calamity shall fall on you, and destruction as a tempest shall be at hand; when tribulation and distress shall come upon you; then shall they call upon me, and I will not hear.*"* There is no help for you now. Your cries of distress, and prayers and entreaties are drowned in the thundering din of the rushing waters: as our Lord prophe-

* Prov. i., 24.

sied. "*Upon the earth distress of nations, men withering away for fear, by reason of the confusion of the roaring of the sea, and of the waves.*"*

What is that which is glimmering white like a sail upon the waves? Can it be a friendly ship coming to your rescue? Hark! Tramp, tramp, over land, over sea. Why does that sound send a shuddering thrill of horror through every nerve? 'Tis no sail. 'Tis a pale horse, and he that rideth thereon is Death. Tramp! tramp! over land, over sea! Oh! woe betide thee, wretched sinner; thine hour is come. One last cry, and the waters of iniquity have closed over you forever! Oh, God! have mercy on poor sinful men, and according to the multitude of thy tender mercies, blot out their iniquities. If thy people Israel shall have sinned against thee, and thou in thine anger hast delivered them up into the hands of their enemies, and they return to thee with all their heart, and confessing to thy name shall come, and pray, and make supplication to thee, then hear thou in heaven, thy dwelling place, their prayers; and forgive thy people, and have compassion

---

* St. Luke xxi., 25.

upon them, and help thy servants whom thou hast redeemed by thy precious blood. What answer dost thou make, O dearest Lord?—"*He that heareth you heareth me.*"*

Thy words, O Jesus, are truth and life. Thou hast commanded thy priests, the ministers of thy word, to speak in thy name; to stand in the path of sinners on the way to destruction, and make thy voice to be heard, ("*Arise! thou that sleepest, and awake from the dead!*") as thou didst to the only son of the widow of Nain. "*Be not deceived,*" says the holy Apostle in the Epistle of this day. "*God is not mocked.*" "*He that despiseth you despiseth me.*"† In the name of God, then, obedient to the charge which I, although unworthy, have received from the Lord Jesus, I say unto you, **arise! Arise from** those disastrous habits of sin, which are dragging you down to death and hell. Abandon, once for all, those horrid haunts of vice and immorality. Put away all those obscenities, evil speakings, and cursings, from your lips; of the which I tell you, as has been already foretold you, that they who do

* St. Luke x., 16. † St. Luke x., 16.

such things, shall not obtain the kingdom of God. Young man, I say unto thee, arise!

Oh! wretched parents, whose miserable home is a very school of Satan to your hapless children; whose daily lives are as an open book before their eyes, every leaf of which is blotted and blurred with drunkenness and disorder—I say unto you, oh, wicked father, oh, slothful mother, arise! You, young woman, over whose head ruin and shame are hanging, arise! send that young man away to-night.

You who have dealt out disgrace, dirt, delirium tremens, ruin, and the wrath of God, by the measure, to your poor fellow sinner, and upon whose guilty head will fall a double weight of woe—I say unto *you*, arise! turn to the Lord, and perhaps he will have mercy upon you. Do penance, do penance! and think not to say within your hearts: We have Abraham for our father; we have the Church for our mother—she will watch over us Catholics, and before it is too late, snatch us from the jaws of hell. I say unto you, sinner, you are deceiving yourself with a lie, and your supine indifference proves you to be of that unhappy number described in Holy Writ, who resisted so long to the Divine call, that, hardened in iniquity, God gave them over to believe a lie. Thus, instead of your faith saving you, it will only be a surer cause of your damnation. Oh! you hope in the mercy of God. Poor soul! God, notwithstanding his mercy, permitted you to fall into your present deplorable state. Why shall he not permit you to fall into eternal death, which, howsoever terrible and hopeless, is not so bad, so evil after all, as your spiritual death: for so say the Doctors of Holy Church. "The punishment of sin is less than the guilt."

Between spiritual and eternal death there is but a step—taken every day by one or another in this sinful world—and that is the death of the body; and if it happens to you to-day, without doubt, without remedy or resource, you will find yourself eternally lost; which may God avert from every one of you. Amen.

SERMON VI.

THE LOVE OF GOD.

"And one of them, a doctor of the law, asked him, tempting him: Master, which is the great commandment of the law? Jesus said to him: Thou shalt love the Lord thy God with thy whole heart, and with thy whole soul and with thy whole mind."—St. Matt. xxii., 35–37.

(From the Gospel for the 17th Sunday after Pent.)

This doctor of the law had no good motive in asking his question. He was full of malice, and desired, not to learn any thing good himself, but to entrap our Lord. But God knows how to draw good out of evil. Though the lawyer's intention was bad, his question was a good one; the very best question that he could have asked, and the answer to it one of vast importance to us, involving all our interests for eternity. Let us to-day consider well the meaning of the answer given by our Blessed Saviour in the words of the text. In the first place, what does he mean by the love of God? and in the second, what degree of this love must we practise?

What is the love of God, or in what does it consist? Many have a false idea of it. They think it is exactly the same as earthly love, the love of relations or friends. They know what that kind of love is. They exercise it without difficulty. Why? because it is spontaneous; it is a flowing out of the heart, an emotion or feeling. They cannot *feel* the same love for God as for their friends, and therefore they conclude it is of no use to try to love God. They make a great mistake. God is a pure spirit, not to be seen, heard, or taken notice of by the senses, and therefore, in the very nature of things, He cannot always be loved with that same emotion or feeling that springs up in our hearts, without effort, toward our neighbors and friends of flesh and blood. Indeed God, considered as an infinite being, with all his vast and unlimited perfections, seems in some way separated from us and our thoughts, which makes a difficulty in feeling emotions of love to Him. The essence of the love of God is not in emotion or feeling, but in our reason and will. Faith reveals Him to us, and we acknowledge Him with our reason to be infinitely wise and infinitely good, and worthy of all our love. The true love of God consists, then, in acknowledging Him with our reason to be what He is, and in the will to do that which is pleasing to Him.

The other kind of love—of feeling—may accompany this true love of God or it may not. It is of no consequence whether it does or not. We have no right to expect it, for God will grant it just as far as He sees good for us and no farther. It will come, generally, as the result of habits of virtue, of a long course of action, in imitation of His holy perfections. We must learn to know Him and prize Him in order to feel love for Him.

That this is the true idea of the love of God is clear from the Holy Scriptures. In the Gospel of St. John it is thus described: *"For this is the charity of God, that we keep his commandments."* It is not said: The love of God is in a delightful feeling that possesses one without any effort on his part. That would be very pleasant and very easy. No; that is not said. But the meaning of what is said is, that the love of God is in the will and determination to keep his commandments. In another place it is said in plain terms: "*He that hath my commandments and keepeth them, he it is that loveth me.*" As much as to say: If your mind and will are directed to me in such a way that you keep my commandments, don't be worried or afraid, you do most truly love me. Now this ought to console any one who really and truly wants to love God, for we see that it lies in his power to do so. He need not go into raptures of fervor. He need not fly in the air in an ecstasy. He need not see visions or work wonders. He need not practise extraordinary fasting or austerity, or spend whole nights in prayer. He need only have a determination, let him feel well or ill, that he will honestly and sincerely act so as to be agreeable to God, and he loves Him. Let him go on acting in that way and he will soon love Him exceedingly, far more than any thing in this world. Another argument that proves conclusively that this is the true love of God, comes from this very command of our Lord Jesus Christ: "*Thou shalt love the Lord thy God with thy whole heart, and with thy whole soul, and with thy whole mind.*" The love of God is commanded. Now God commands nothing impossible, nothing, in short, which is very difficult to set about. As he is a God of infinite goodness and love, the bare idea of such a thing is wholly repugnant to right reason and common sense. If He had commanded us to exercise a sensible love—one of feeling— we might justly complain and say: I cannot fulfil it; that is a thing beyond my control. We have to set about a practical love—keeping his commandments, that is a business we can give our mind and attention to, as we would to farming, building, doctoring, or any other business. If a man will set about the business of practically acting according to the will of God, he will add every day to his stock of love and to his merit in heaven. This is a rich mine; it is inexhaustible; out of this mine is drawn the pure gold of charity to God, richer and more abundant than all the mines of California or Australia.

But what degree of this love must we exercise in order to obtain everlasting life? A high degree of it: not a low measure of it, but a large and liberal one if we would make our calling and election sure. Our Lord's answer to the question indicates that beyond mistake: "*Thou shalt love the Lord thy God with all thy heart and all thy soul and all thy mind.*" That sounds strong; that sounds hard; words could hardly be put together to convey a stronger meaning. It would seem to mean that all our thoughts and desires and actions should be engrossed and taken up with God and eternity, so as to leave room for nothing else. This would indeed be hard, and it would be absurd, considering the order of things which God has established in the world. God created us to live in society and the most of us for society, to play our part in it, to bring up families of children—to put bread and butter in their mouths, and clothes on their backs. We cannot then abandon the world, and we must devote our attention to its affairs: we must give a reasonable attention to do them well, for the advantage of ourselves and those connected with us. What is the meaning, then, of loving with one's whole heart and soul and mind?

We must have our will and determination directed in the first place to God and to keeping his commandments, leaving every thing else to the second place. A man must be determined to keep God's commandments in spite of every obstacle, in spite of every temptation. He must be determined to keep them all, that is, at least, to avoid every mortal sin. He must be determined not only for the present, but so long as the breath is in his body. If he falls short of this, he does not love God with all his heart and soul and mind; he does not do what is necessary to obtain everlasting life, and he will not obtain it.

It is required by God, as an essential condition to our salvation, that we should be habitually in the determination to keep free from every mortal sin. What can be more just? We acknowledge him as our Creator, and as infinitely wise and infinitely good. He is rightly our sovereign Lord and Master, and can command what he chooses—there is an equal obligation on our part to obey him. Is it asking much, that we shall be habitually obedient? Any thing short of this he could not require—we could not expect. Is it for Him to be dependent upon our moods and humors, finding us true to-day and false to-morrow?

Oh! you say, is that all that is required of us to insure our salvation—to keep clear of mortal sin? That is nothing new; we knew that all along; to go that far is not much; we can do that easily enough. Can you, indeed? Perhaps it is easy enough to avoid mortal sin for a time, when there is fervor, or particular grace, or little temptation; but is it easy to do so for one's whole life? Is it easy to do so when one's fervor is worn off, and distractions of all kinds occupy the mind, and when in this state strong temptations beset one? Whoever says this, shows that he has little knowledge of himself, and little experience in affairs of the soul. You may avoid sin a little while, but you will fall, as sure as you live, if your mind is not set against sin, actively and habitually, so as to turn away from it with horror in the moment of temptation. No; in order not to fall, our whole life must be directed toward God. The eternal truths, heaven, hell, death, judgment, must pass frequently through our minds and take up our thoughts. In the words of Scripture, we must keep our lamps trimmed, and well supplied with oil, lest they go out. Our souls must be trimmed with holy meditations, and the oil of good works supplied in abundance must keep the flame of love to God burning brightly in our hearts, or else it will go out. It will fade away gradually for want of nourishment, until it is gone. We cannot keep clear even of mortal sin, unless we are thoroughly in earnest about it, and make a business of it. When our Lord says, " Love the Lord thy God with thy whole heart and thy whole soul, and thy whole mind," He means to say: Put your heart and soul in the business of your salvation. Make a sure thing of it by the energy and determination you apply to it.

" *The children of this world are wiser*," says the Lord, "*than the children of light.*" All their prudence and skill is laid out to succeed in their business, to scrape together what they consider desirable for this life. If any thing like the same prudence and skill were exercised in serving God, salvation would be an easy thing. If you want to be saved, you must put your souls in it. You all know what the meaning of putting your souls in a thing is. It is a saying used every day. 'His soul is in his business; his soul is in study; her soul is in fashion, in her family.' How the poor girl at service, when she wants to please her mistress, puts her soul in her work! What delight she takes in having every thing clean and in order! When she gets a compliment for her skill or industry, what heartfelt pleasure it gives her! Her continual study is to please in every way. How the young man puts his soul in pleasure sometimes! Every cent he can earn is spent in the saloon, the circus, the theatre. Let him earn a little **money**, he breaks off work until it is all squandered. Sundays, holidays, all are consumed in his darling occupations of **drinking and** making merry. In his pursuit of pleasure, God, reputation, health, must all give way. Nothing is allowed to put any obstacle in his headlong career. So it is with the covetous man. Money is his sole delight. His heart is satisfied with the pleasure of hoarding it, the pleasure of getting more and more. He has more than he knows what **to do** with: that makes **no** difference. He wants still more. He has nothing to give away. He **can't** afford this, he can't afford that. He has no time for amusement; business, mortgages, interest, that's all the amusement he cares for. Anxious and fretful for little losses, he wears out his life, and leaves his property for somebody else to spend, perhaps to be a curse to some worthless relation. He has put his soul in his money-bags.

We see people every day whose souls are so taken up with the world, that they can't even give a thought to any thing that lies beyond it. They verify the words of Scripture: "*Let us eat, drink, and be merry, for to-morrow we die,*" that is, they would be glad to persuade themselves, if they could, that they have no souls, and are determined to act practically on these suppositions. Now, in the same way that these poor miserable creatures put their souls in business, pleasure, love of money, or worldly ease and comfort, put yours in the business of your salvation. Make it your study to please God. Don't say: how little can I do and get off with it? but, how much can I do? What opportunity, what golden opportunity offers, to do something to please God?

Ah! there are plenty of opportunities for all who wish to avail themselves of them. The poor man can strive to do his duty, by honest industry supporting his family, setting them a good example. He has a good deal to put up with, in the shape of poverty, sickness, cold, hunger, and fatigue. He can love God with his whole soul, by putting up with these things patiently. These things are his money, with which he may be sure of purchasing the kingdom of heaven.

The rich man, if his soul is in his salvation, considers himself as God's trustee, not to dispose of the wealth God allots him as he pleases, but to advance His kingdom and the salvation of souls. He does not care so much for pampering his body, making a show, or heaping up riches for his heirs, but is satisfied with a competence and means enough to live according to his station; the rest he spends in promoting true and deserving objects of charity. He likes to imitate Jesus Christ in helping the poor and the sick, keeping a free bed in the hospital, sustaining institutions for the relief of orphans, the insane, and all who need it. He likes to help a deserving young man, when he finds one of the sort, to become a priest in the church of God. He don't consider it entirely the business of the priest to build churches, wearing himself out to collect the means, and that from the hard earnings of the poor, but steps forth promptly, and takes his full share of the expense and the labor attending such enterprises. When he finds a hard-working priest, zealous for souls, he will stand by him and work with him, only too thankful to get a chance to do something.

In short, if we would make eternal life secure, we must have a spirit of self-sacrifice and devotedness, such as led the holy Martyrs to lay down their lives for the faith—such at least in kind, if not in measure.

Oh! my brethren, how happy is the man who cherishes such a principle in his heart. He is not divided and torn asunder by a continual strife between good and evil. He is not a double dealer. He is not striving to serve two masters. God reigns in his heart, and peace prevails in it. Loss of property cannot take it away, for property is not the main thing in his soul. Neither can loss of friends. He has long been sensible that God is the only true unchangeable friend. Death cannot disturb it—for he is at peace with God, and don't fear death. Oh! why have we not all this spirit? We acknowledge how beautiful it is. We cannot but regret if we have it not. Let us then try for it. Let us begin to-day—by forming a deep and strong resolution that we will not live for the world, or the things of the world, but seek God first of all. That we will really love Him with our whole heart, and that this shall be the business of our lives. Then shall be true of us what is said by the holy Psalmist: "*Blessed is the man who hath not walked in the counsel of the ungodly, nor stood in the way of sinners, nor sat in the chair of pestilence. But his will is in the law of the Lord and on his law he shall meditate day and night. And he shall be like the tree that is planted near the running waters, which shall bring forth its fruit in due season, and his leaf shall not fall off, and all whatsoever he shall do shall prosper.*" Then all shall prosper with us here below, for all things shall speed our way to that world above, where, without effort, in a perfect manner, to our unbounded joy, we shall love God with our whole heart and soul, and mind, and strength.

SERMON VII.

KEEPING THE LAW NOT IMPOSSIBLE.

"I can do all things in Him who strengtheneth me."
Phil. vi., 13.

If I am not mistaken, a very great number of the sins that men commit, are committed through hopelessness. The pleasures of sin are by no means unmixed. Indeed, sin is a hard master; and all who practice it find it so. I never met a man who said it was a good thing, or that it made him happy. On the contrary, all lament it, and say that it makes them miserable. Why then, do they commit it? Very often, I am persuaded, because they think they have no power to resist it. They feel in themselves strong passions; they have yielded to them in times past, they see that others yield to them, and so they come to think it impossible not to yield to them. The law of God is too difficult, they say. It is impossible to keep it. It may do for priests or nuns who are cut off from the world, or for women, or for the old, or for children, but for us who mix in the world, whose blood is warm, and whose passions are strong, it is too high and pure. It is all very well to talk about; it is all very well to hold up a high standard to us, but you must not expect us to attain it. The utmost that you can expect of us is to stop sinning, now and then, and make the proper acknowledgments to God by going to confession, but actually to try not to sin, to keep on endeavoring not to sin at any time, or under any circumstances, that is impossible, or at least so extremely difficult that, practically speaking, it is impossible. Are there none of you, my brethren, who recognize this as the secret language of your hearts? Is there not an impression in your minds that the law of God is too strict? or at least that it is too strict for you, and that you cannot keep it? If so, do not harbor it. It is a fatal error. No: it is not impossible to keep God's law. It is not impossible to keep from mortal sin. It is, I admit, impossible to keep from every venial sin, though even here we can do a great deal if we try. Such is the frailty of human nature that even the best men as time goes on fall into some slight faults, only the blessed Virgin having been able, as we believe, to pass a whole life without even in the smallest thing offending God. But it is possible for all of us to keep from mortal sin, at all times and under all circumstances. This, I think, you will acknowledge when you consider the character of God, the nature of God's law, and the power of God's grace which is promised to us.

I say the character of God is a pledge of our ability to keep from mortal sin. God requires us to be free from mortal sin, and He requires it under the severest penalties, and therefore it must be possible for us. You may say, "God requires us to be free from venial sin too, and yet you have just said we cannot avoid every venial sin." But the case is far different. A venial sin does not separate us from God, and does not receive extreme punishment from Him—nay, those venial sins which even good men commit, and which are only in small part voluntary, are very easily forgiven—but a mortal sin cuts us off entirely from God, and deserves eternal punishment. You know, one mortal sin is enough to damn a man—one single sin of drunkenness, for instance, or impurity; a cherished hatred, a false oath, or an act of grave injustice. One such sin is sufficient to sink a man in hell, and although we know very little in particular of the torments of hell, we have every reason to believe that they are most bitter, and we know that they are eternal. Now can it be thought that a being of justice and goodness, as we know God to be, would inflict so extreme a punishment for an offence which was unavoidable, or could only be avoided with the utmost difficulty? Holy Scripture sends us to an earthly parent for an example of that tenderness and affection which we are to expect from our Heavenly Father. "*If you being evil know how to give good gifts to your children, how much more will your Father who is in heaven, give good things to them that ask him.*"* What would be thought of an earthly father who laid upon his son a command which it was all but impossible for him to comply with, and then punished him with the utmost

---

* St. Matt., vii., 11.

rigor for not fulfilling it? You would not call that man a father, but a tyrant; a tyrant like Pharaoh, who would not give straw to the children of Israel, and yet set taskmasters over them to exact of them the full measure of bricks as when straw had been given them. Why, if you were going along the street and saw a man whipping unmercifully an overloaded horse, you would not bear it patiently. And would you attribute conduct so disgraceful among men to our Father in heaven? God forbid! Far be such a thought from us! It is not so. We must not think it. At least we cannot think it as long as we remain Catholics, for when the earlier Protestants proclaimed the shocking doctrine that though God punished men for disobeying his law, man was really unable to obey it, the Church branded the doctrine as a heresy to be abhorred of all men, as most false in itself, and most injurious to God. No; God loves his creatures far more than we conceive of. He does not desire the death of a sinner. He wills truly the salvation of all men. His goodness and mercy, his truth and justice, are all so many infallible guarantees of our ability to keep his law. He would not have given us his law unless He had meant us to keep it. He would not punish us so severely for breaking it, unless our breaking it was an **act** of deliberate, wilful, determined rebellion.

But there is another source from which I draw the conclusion that it is possible to keep the law of God—from the nature of the law itself. The law of God is of such a nature that, for the most part, in order to commit mortal sin, it is necessary to do or to leave undone some external act, which of its own nature it is entirely in our power to do or not to do. For instance, the law says, "*Thou shalt not steal:*" now to steal you have got to put your hand into your neighbor's pocket. The law says: "*Thou shalt do no murder;*" to murder you must stretch out your hand against your neighbor's life. Nay, it requires ordinarily several external actions before a mortal sin is consummated. Thus the thief has his precautions to take, and his plans to lay. The drunkard has to seek the occasion. He seeks the grog-shop. Every step he takes is a separate act. When he gets there it is not the first glass that makes him drunk. He drinks again and again, and it is only after all these different and repeated actions that he falls into the mortal sin of drunkeness. Now here you see are external acts—acts in which the hand, the foot, the lips are concerned, and which, therefore, it is perfectly in our power to do or to let alone. This requires no proof, but admits of a striking illustration. You have heard of the great sufferings of the martyrs; how some of them were stoned to death, others flayed alive, others crucified, others torn to pieces by wild beasts, others burned to death. Now what was it all about? You answer, 'They suffered because they would not deny Christ.' Very well; but how were they required to deny Christ? What was it they were required to do? I will tell you. Sometimes they were required to take a few grains of incense and throw it on the altar of Jupiter; that would have been enough to have saved them from their sufferings. They need not have said, 'I renounce Christ;' only to have taken the incense would have been sufficient. Sometimes they were required to tread on the Cross. Sometimes to swear by the genius of the Roman emperor; that was all. And the fire was kindled to make them do these things;

6*

but they would not. The flames leaped upon them, but not a foot would they lift from the ground. Their hands were burnt to the bone, but no incense would they touch. The marrow of their bones melted in the heat, and forced from them a cry of agony, but the name of the emperor's tutelary genius did not pass their lips. Now will you tell me that you cannot help doing what the martyrs would not do to save them from death? They had a fire before them and a scourge behind them, and they refused; and you say you cannot help yourself when you are under no external violence whatever! They died rather than lift a hand to do a forbidden thing; have you not the same power over your hand that they had? They died rather than utter a sinful word; have you not as much power over your tongue as they? Indeed you have, for you control both one and the other whenever you will. I say there is no sinner whose conduct does not show that his actions are perfectly in his own power. The thief waits for the night to carry on his trade; during the day he is honest enough. The greatest libertine knows how to behave himself in the presence of a high-born and virtuous female. And even that vice which men say it is most difficult of all to restrain when once the habit is formed—profane swearing—you know how to restrain it when you will, for even the heaviest curser and swearer ceases from his oaths before the priest, or any other friend whom he greatly respects. Now, if you can stop cursing before the priest, why can you not before your wife and children? If you can be chaste in the presence of a virtuous female, why can you not be chaste everywhere? If you can be honest when the eye of man is on you, why can you not be honest when no eye sees you but that of God?

'But' some one may say, 'there is a class of sins to which the remarks you have made do not apply, that is, sins of thought. You must admit that they are of such a nature that it is all but impossible not to commit them.' No, I do not admit it. I acknowledge that sins of thought are more difficult to guard against than sins of action; but I do not acknowledge that it is impossible to guard against them. To prove this I have only to remind you that an evil thought is no sin until we give *consent* to it. To keep always free from evil thoughts may be impossible, because the imagination is in its nature so volatile, that but few men have it in control; but though it be not possible to restrain the imagination, it is always possible to restrain the will. In order for the will to consent to evil it is necessary both to *know* and to *choose*, and therefore from the nature of the thing one can never fall into sin neither inevitably or unawares. And besides, the will has a powerful ally in the conscience, whose province it is to keep us from sin and to reproach us when we do sin—so that it is scarcely possible, for one who habitually tries to keep free from mortal sin, to fall into it without his conscience giving a distinct and unmistakable report. And this is so certain that spiritual writers say that a person of good life and tender conscience, who is distressed with the uncertainty whether or no he has given consent to an evil temptation, ought to banish that anxiety altogether and to be sure that he has not consented. But suppose these evil temptations are importunate, and remain in the soul even when we resist them, and try to turn from them? No matter. They do not become sins on that account; nay, they become the occasion of acts of great virtue. It is related in the life of St. Catherine of Sienna that on one occasion that pure virgin's soul was assailed by the most horrible temptations of the devil. They lasted for a long time, and after the conflict our Saviour appeared to her with a serene countenance. "O my Divine Spouse," she said, "Where wast thou when I was enduring these conflicts?" "In thy soul," he replied. "What, with all these filthy abominations?" "Yes, they were displeasing and painful to thee; this therefore was thy merit, and thy victory was owing to my presence." So that we see even here where the danger is greatest, the law of God exacts of us nothing but what in its own nature is in our power to do or not to do.

But if you wish another proof of your ability to keep God's law, I allege the *power of his grace*. I can imagine an objector saying: 'You have not touched the real difficulty after all. The difficulty is not on God's side; no doubt He is good and holy. Neither are the requirements of his law so very hard. The difficulty is in us. We are fallen by nature. We have sinned after baptism. We are so weak, so frail, that to us continued observance of the divine commandments is impossible.' No, my brethren, neither is this true. It is not true from the mouth of any man; least of all from the mouth of a Christian. "*No temptation,*" says the Apostle, "*hath taken hold of you but such as is human. And God is faithful, who will not suffer you to be tempted above that which you are able; but will also with the temptation make a way of escape that you may be able to bear it.*"* The weakest and frailest are strong enough with God's grace, and this grace He is ready to give to those that need it. At all times and in all places He has been ready to give his grace to them that need it, but especially is this true under the gospel. The Holy Scriptures make this the distinguishing characteristic of the times of the gospel that they shall abound in grace. "*Take courage, and fear not,*" the prophet says, in anticipation of the time when Christ should come in the flesh, "*Behold God will come and save you. Then shall the eyes of the blind be opened, and the ears of the deaf unstopped. Then shall the lame man leap as an hart, and the tongue of*

* 1 Cor. x., 13.

the dumb shall be free; for waters are broken out of the desert, and streams in the wilderness. And that which was dry land shall become a pool, and the thirsty land springs of water."*
Such was the promise, hundreds of years before Christ, of a time of peace, of happiness and grace; and when our Lord was come, He published that the good time had indeed arrived: "*The spirit of the Lord hath anointed me to preach the gospel to the poor. He hath sent me to heal the contrite of heart. To preach deliverance to the captive, and sight to the blind, to set at liberty them that are bruised, to preach the acceptable year of the Lord.*" Yes, the great time has come; the cool of the day; the evening of the world; the time when labor is light and reward abundant. Oh, my brethren, you know not what a privilege it is to be a Christian! You enter a church. You see a priest in his confessional. A penitent is kneeling at his feet. The sight makes but little impression on you, for you are accustomed to it, but this is that "*fountain*" promised by the prophet "*to the house of David and to the inhabitants of Jerusalem, for the washing of the*

* Is. xxxv., 4—7.

sinner;" a fountain that flows from the Saviour's side, and not only cleanses, but strengthens and makes alive. You pass an altar. The priest is giving communion. Stop! it is the Lord himself! the bread of angels! the wine of virgins! the food "*whereof if a man eat he shall live forever.*" And not only in the Church do you find grace. It follows you home. You shut your door behind you, and your Father in heaven waits to hear and grant your prayer. Nay, at all times God is with you, for you are the temple of God, and He sits on the throne of your heart to scatter his grace on you whenever and wherever you ask Him. Do not say, then, Christian, that you are unable to do what God requires of you. It is a sin of black ingratitude to say so. Even if it were impossible for others to keep the law of God, it is not for you. He hath not done to every nation as he hath done to you. When the patriarch Jacob was dying, he blessed all his children, but his richest blessing was for Joseph. So God has blessed all the children of his hand, but you, Christian, are the Joseph whom He hath loved more than all his other sons. To others He hath given of "*the dew of heaven,*" and "*the fatness of the earth*," but you "*He hath blessed with all spiritual blessings in Christ.*"

Away, then, with the notion, that obedience to the commandments of God is impracticable. A notion dishonorable to God and to ourselves, It is possible to keep free from mortal sin—for all—at all times, under all temptations. Nay, I will say more. It is on the whole, easier to live a life of Christian obedience, than a life of sin. I say ' on the whole,' for I do not deny that here and there in particular cases, it is harder to do right than wrong, but taking life all through, one who restrains his passions will have less trouble than one who indulges them. Heroic actions are not required of us every day. In order to be a Christian, it is not necessary to be always high-strung and enthusiastic. It is not necessary to be a devotee, to adopt set and precise ways, to take up with hypocrisy and cant—in a word, to be unmanly. It is just, for the most part, the most matter of fact, the most practical, the most simple and straight-forward thing in the world. It is to be a man of principle. It is to have a serious, abiding purpose to do our duty. It is to be full of courage; not the courage of the braggart, but the courage of the soldier—the courage that thrives under opposition, and survives defeat, the courage that takes the means to secure success—vigilance, humility, steadfastness and prayer. Before this, all difficulties vanish, and this is what we want most of all. It is amazing how little courage there is in the world. We are like the servant of Eliseus, the prophet, who, when he awoke in the morning, and saw the great army that had been sent by the King of Syria to take his master, said, "*Alas, alas, alas, my lord; what shall we do!*" But Eliseus showed him another army—the army of angels ranged on the mountain, with chariots of fire and horses of fire, ready to fight for the servants of God, and he said, "*Fear not: for there are more with us than with them.*"* Why should we fear? Christianity is no new thing. The path of Christian obedience is not an untried path. Thousands have trod it and are now enjoying their reward. God, and the angels, and the saints, are on our side. And there are multitudes of faithful souls in the world who are fighting the good fight, and keeping their souls

---

* 4 Kings. vi., 15—17.

unsullied. We cannot distinguish them now, but one day we shall know them. Oh! let us join them. Yes, we will make our resolution now. Others may guide themselves by pleasure or expediency; we will adopt the language of the Psalmist: *"Thy word is a lamp to my feet, and a light to my paths."** We will be Christians not in name, but in deed. Not for a time only, but always. One thought shall cheer us in sadness and nerve us in weakness, *" I have sworn and am determined to keep the judgments of thy justice."*

* Psalm cxviii., 105.

SERMON VIII.

THE TWO STANDARDS.

"No man can serve two masters."—St. Matt., vi. 24.

(From the Gospel of the 14th Sunday after Pent.)

There are two hostile camps pitched on the surface of the earth, and two great armies engaged in warfare against each other. The chiefs of these two armies are Jesus Christ and Satan. The war between them is not a new one. It began in heaven, when Lucifer and his companions rebelled against God. It broke out in a more deadly and decisive manner, when Jesus Christ erected his standard on Mt. Calvary, and from his Cross triumphed over the devil, while Satan, enraged at his defeat, summoned all his forces from earth and hell to an eternal war against the Cross.

This is a war in which every one must take part. Here no one can remain neutral; either for the Cross or against it—a soldier of Christ or a servant of the devil. You must choose your side. Which, then, do you take? Will you have Christ or Lucifer for your king? In the name of Jesus Christ, I call on you to renounce the infamous service of the devil for ever, and enroll yourself under the standard of the Cross, and I promise to give you good reasons for doing so. Listen, then, and make your decision. If the devil has the best claim, and offers the highest price, then follow him, and take his lot in this world and in eternity. But consider well what you have to look for, beforehand. If Jesus Christ is your rightful Lord, and heaven is worth having, then come out boldly on his side, and renounce the devil once for all. You cannot serve both, you must serve one; and the one whom you serve on this earth, will have possession of you for all eternity.

Survey, then, the two camps, the two standards, the two kings. On Mount Calvary see the Cross, the standard of salvation, rising above the camp of Jesus Christ. Look on the

King who rules in this camp! Regard his features: they are full of majesty and humility, of power and of love, of authority and of compassion. Around Him the Blessed Virgin, the apostles, martyrs and confessors, all the saints and all the righteous, are grouped; and from his Cross He sends out his messengers into all the world, inviting all men to share his humility, self-denial, and suffering in this world, and his everlasting kingdom in the next.

Now turn your eyes toward the other camp. It lies near the city of Babylon, the city of this world, a city of idolatry, sensuality, and worldly pomp. In the midst of it, Satan is seated on a high and burning throne, his features full of melancholy, pride and cruelty, surrounded by his demons, his false priests, and the multitude of his worshippers. He also sends his messengers through the earth, offering honors, pleasures, and riches here, and the fire of hell hereafter, to those who enlist in his service.

Unhappy man! soldier of Christ by baptism! have these ministers of Satan persuaded you to renounce your lawful standard, and enlist under that of the devil? Have you been persuaded by some worldly bribe, some passing pleasure, to renounce God and heaven, and to receive the black brand of mortal sin in your soul, the mark of your allegiance to the devil? What have you done? What master is this, to whom you have sold yourself? What have you to expect in his service? Listen to me, and I will prove to you that you have sold yourself to a detestable tyrant and usurper; that you have cast in your lot with a desperate cause, and that everlasting ruin is the only wages you will ever get.

Satan is a detestable usurper. What right has he to reign in this world? What right has he to your soul, or to your service? Did he create the world, or make you? Has he conferred any benefit on the human race, that he is entitled to the gratitude and obedience of men? He is a miserable rebel against God, an outcast from heaven, the great enemy of mankind. He is the author of sin, misery, and death. He became master of your soul by mortal sin. He seduced you to offend God by lying promises, and treacherously got possession of your heart. Is he not then a usurper?

He is also a cruel tyrant. Satan tyrannizes

over the soul which is subject to him, by making it a slave to its **passions**. He makes it sweat and toil like a negro slave, fast, and watch, and deny itself, like a hermit, in the service of **these** cruel taskmasters. One he **forces** to labor night and day for a lifetime, to scrape up a little money which he has no time to enjoy. Another he compels to sacrifice health, reputation, and fortune, to the gratification of **lust**. A third he turns into a beast by drunkenness. He tyrannizes over his subjects, also, by **continual and insupportable** torments of conscience. They have none of that peace and tranquillity which the servants of God enjoy, but a horrible foretaste of the pains of hell, in the incessant gnawings of a guilty conscience, and the continual fear of eternal damnation.

The service of **Satan is odious**, on account of the companions with whom you must associate. You become the associate of demons, **murderers, thieves, harlots, drunkards,** and villains of every hue. The promises which the **devil** holds out to you are all false, and his words all delusive. He holds out to you an illusory hope of liberty and happiness, and deceives you with glittering but unreal pictures of future enjoyment. For these you renounce Christian self-denial; for these you throw down the Cross of Christ, abandon the straight and narrow way, and sacrifice your hopes of heaven. But the devil will disappoint you. The pleasure he will give you will leave behind in your heart only bitterness and disgust. You will have to endure in his service labors and sufferings more than enough to make you a saint, if you performed them for God. You threw down the cross which God placed on your shoulders. It was a light cross, and was exactly measured for your size and strength. It was a cross full of blessings and graces, and if you had carried it courageously up the narrow way of life, after a time it would have supported you, and you would have been borne up by it to the gate of heaven. But you threw it down, because it was too heavy and galling, and turned from the steep path of virtue to the downward, flowery road of sin. Immediately the devil came up behind you, and fastened on your back an immense cross of rough, unhewn timber. Loaded with this devil's cross, you are stumbling along the way of perdition toward the mouth of hell, into which you will fall at death, with **the** heavy burden of your sins on your back to press you down, and crush you forever beneath its weight. Such is the hard and bitter slavery to which you have bound yourself under this detestable tyrant.

Moreover, his cause is a desperate one. A certain and ignominious defeat, from which he will never more arise, awaits him. He has already been conquered. Jesus Christ met him once in single combat in the desert, and **put** him to an ignominious **flight**. Afterwards, on the cross, He gained a still more signal and decisive victory over him, and made him serve by his own plan for our Lord's destruction, as an instrument for accomplishing our salvation. The Blessed Virgin has trampled on the head of this malicious serpent. All the saints and martyrs have triumphed over him, and the weakest Christian child can put him to flight, by resisting his temptations—by breathing **a little prayer, or by** making the sign of the cross. **He is** a weak and miserable coward. His cause is already desperate and lost. And although God allows him a certain liberty to tempt and trouble the world for a short time, the day of judgment is fast approaching, in which Jesus Christ will put him to shame before the whole universe, and cast him, together with all those who follow his standard, into the burning abyss of hell.

Such is a true picture of Lucifer, of his services, and of the reward which awaits his followers. Are you not ashamed, then, O false Christian! to have renounced your allegiance to your rightful Lord, for the service of such a master, who trembles at the very name of Jesus Christ?

In the churches of the middle ages the statue of the martyr St. Christopher was frequently sculptured, carrying, in accordance with his name which signifies Christ-bearer, the infant Jesus on his shoulder. As his real history was unknown, the poetic fancy of that period invented several beautiful legends about it, of which the following is one:

"A heathen youth of gigantic size and strength determined to seek out the strongest man in the world, and serve him. After many inquiries, he engaged himself to a Christian prince, who was famous for prowess and warlike achievements. He served him contentedly for a while, but at length, observing that he often made the sign of the cross, he asked him the meaning of his doing so. The prince told him it was to keep off the devil. The youth asked him who the devil was, and if he was afraid of him. He told him that the devil was a wicked being, more powerful than any man, and that he feared him greatly. 'If that is the case,' said the youth, 'I will serve you no longer, but I will serve the devil, because he is the strongest.' Immediately he set out to seek for him, and passing through a forest was accosted by a dark-looking personage who asked him what he was looking for, and on receiving his his answer, replied: 'I am the devil you are seeking, follow me if you wish to enter my service.' So saying, he went on, followed by the youth, toward a certain city. As they drew near the city, the devil turned aside from the highway, and took a bye-road which was much more circuitous. The youth asked him why he did not keep the high-road. 'Do you not see,' said the devil, 'that crucifix? I do not wish to pass it.' 'What is a crucifix?' said the youth. 'The image of my greatest enemy, who once conquered me,' replied the devil. 'Farewell,' said the youth; 'if you are afraid of Him who hangs on that cross, I shall leave you, and serve Him, because he is stronger than you.' So saying, he went in search of Jesus Christ, and having stopped at a monastery, and asked the way to find Him, was instructed, baptized by the name of Christopher, and became a martyr."

Now, dear Christian, you are a Christopher, a Christ-bearer, for you have the image of Christ stamped in your soul in baptism. You are bound to serve the most powerful, and not only the most powerful, but the best master; the one who has the best right to your services, whose service is the most honorable, whose rewards are the greatest, and whose final victory is certain. Listen to me now, and I will show you that this Prince is Jesus Christ.

Jesus Christ is our lawful King.

I. By hereditary right. He is the Son of God. In his divine nature He is equal to his Father, and equally with Him the Creator of all things, and therefore our sovereign Lord. In his human nature, He is the first begotten Son of his Father, the heir of all things, and in a special sense, the chief of the human race.

II. By purchase. By Adam's sin, the special gifts which God had given to him and his posterity—integrity of nature, sanctifying grace, paradise and the title to heaven—were forfeited. Mankind fell from a free to a servile condition. Jesus Christ, by a compact with the eternal Father, and by pledging His life for us, has purchased his right over us.

III. By redemption. He has redeemed us by his blood, from exile and slavery, and restored to us our forfeited inheritance of grace and eternal life.

IV. By conquest. When the whole world was subject to the usurped tyranny of Satan, He made war on him, conquered him, and wrested our souls from his possession. As subjects of a conquered empire, we are therefore subject to the dominion of our conqueror.

V. By our own election. We have freely chosen his service, when we were confirmed and ratified our baptismal vows, and a thousand times we have offered ourselves to his service, and sworn allegiance to Him.

His service is glorious. Because He is the greatest and wisest of all princes; because angels and saints are our companions; because his service consists in performing great and heroic actions, warring against vice, overcoming self, practising virtue, doing good, and conquering the world, the flesh and the devil. It is happy and delightful, because of peace of conscience, the friendship of God, and the consolations of divine grace. These are a sort of bounty or earnest-money given now; but the real reward is eternal life, to be given hereafter.

Jesus Christ is certain to obtain the victory and to triumph gloriously over all his enemies —over treacherous and cowardly followers within his own camp, that is, bad Christians who preserve the faith but live and die in sin; over all those who are nominally his followers, but who really are fighting under the devil's standard, that is heretics, and schismatics; over infidels, his open enemies among men; over Satan and hell.

Here now are the two chiefs. There are the two standards. This is the war in which every one of you is engaged, on one side or the other? Which side is it? Under what banner have you till now been ranged? Do you belong to the party of Jesus Christ or that of the devil? Do you reply, I am a baptized Christian, marked with the sign of the cross, and a member of the Catholic Church, and therefore a **servant of Jesus Christ?** It is true you are a soldier regularly enlisted and sworn into Christ's army, and wearing his uniform. But the question is, are you a true-hearted, obedient and brave soldier of Jesus Christ, or are you a traitor in the camp, a servant of the devil in the guise of a Christian? Let us see. You call yourself a soldier of Jesus Christ. What are you doing then with the devil's bounty? The devil's bounty is a license to steal, cheat and swindle. What is that pile of bank-notes pilfered from your employer, you dishonest clerk? What is that heap of gold, you bribed judge, you corrupt legislator, you dishonest official, you swindling speculator in government contracts, in public distresses and private miseries? Jesus Christ will tolerate no thieves in his camp. If you are one of these unjust, dishonest, avaricious, overreaching robbers of your neighbors' goods, standing ready to **sell** your voice, your pen, **your vote,** your oath, your conscience, your country, your faith, your soul, your God Himself, for gold, then you have touched the devil's bounty, you are his servant, and a traitor to your colors.

You are a soldier of Jesus Christ, are you? But you have been caught drinking the devil's treat. There, where his sergeants recruit for hell, in those grog-shops whose flaming signs and glaring windows tempt the fool and the unwary; where misery, beggary, despair and death are dealt out to wretched fathers, brutal husbands, ragged, bloated women who are wives and mothers; there you have drained the cup of drunkenness, the pledge of friendship with Satan and all the company of hell.

You are a Christian soldier, are you? But I hear on your lips the devil's passwords, those curses and oaths, those obscene words and profane jests which show that you belong to the devil's camp. Your cursing tongue has betrayed you, false deserter, your speech is the speech of hell, and your presence among the faithful soldiers of Jesus Christ is an offence and a scandal not to be borne by those who have any zeal for the honor of their Lord.

You a Christian soldier?—and flaunting on

the devil's parade-ground, the theatre, the ball-room where the lascivious waltz goes on, the midnight revel of thoughtless and giddy young people, flushed with wine, intoxicated with excitment, **whirled away by the tide of passion**, where they know not and care not, until at length remorse, **disgrace and ruin** tell them where, but too late to save them. These are the pomps of the devil which you renounced and foreswore **at your baptism.** If you take them up again, **you are** an outcast from Jesus Christ, and a servant of the devil.

You dare to call yourself a Christian, and all the while you are living on the devil's pay, feeding on sensuality, plunged overhead in impurity, the miserable, beastly reward that the devil gives to **his followers.** By the law of Moses, those who committed such crimes were to be stoned to death without the camp. Is the camp of Jesus Christ less holy, think you, that an impure man or woman can be tolerated within its sacred precincts?

You pretend to wear the livery of Jesus Christ. What, then, is that badge, what are those insignia you are wearing? They tell that you belong to some secret society, that you have defied the law of the Church, and braved her excommunication. You are then shut out from the sacraments, and not only are you no soldier of Jesus Christ, but you belong to the devil's own body-guard.

Tell me, you pretended soldier of Jesus Christ, where are you on your King's parade days, his Sundays and Festivals, when he requires his servants on earth and his angels in heaven to present themselves in review before him? Where are you during the holy solemnity of the Mass? Absent; your place vacant, and you asleep, or lounging, or doing the devil's work. At the Easter Communion, where are you? You are not to be found, or still worse, you present yourself without that rich and ornamental dress of sanctifying grace, which your king requires, under pain of death. Blush to call yourself a soldier of Jesus Christ, for if you are one, you are a delinquent and a faithless one.

You profess yourself so loudly a Christian soldier, what then are you straggling for, behind your column? Jesus Christ allows no stragglers in his army, and the enemy has ambuscades everywhere to cut them off. These are those heretical churches into which you stray, in ignorance or neglect of Catholic order and discipline. Hasten out of these ambuscades of error, delusion and eternal death. Rejoin your column quickly, and keep within the serried ranks of the Catholic host, or you are lost.

My brave and vaunting Christian warrior, how do your professions of fidelity and courage comport with your conduct when put on guard at night? How have you conducted yourself in temptation? Have you not committed mortal sin, and then given as an excuse that you were tempted by the devil, or overcome by your passions? Have you not said that you could not help cursing when you were angry, drinking when you were urged, giving way to impure inclinations when you were assaulted by them, that you could not keep from mortal sin, because you are so weak? These excuses make you more guilty. They show that you have slept on your post, or kept a careless watch on the enemy, or yielded yourself a prisoner, when you should have fought manfully. It is your very profession as a soldier of Jesus Christ to fight with the world, the flesh and the devil, and you cannot be surprised or vanquished without your own fault. To say that you must sin because the devil tempts you, or that you cannot resist your evil inclinations, is to confess your own shame, and to make it plain, that you are a coward, unworthy of the glorious name of a soldier of Jesus Christ.

I call upon you, then, unworthy and unfaithful followers of Jesus Christ, to renounce your secret and treasonable dealings with the enemy, to cease to act like traitors or poltroons, and to rally again around the standard of salvation. No matter what mortal sin you have on your soul, it is a bond which links you with the devil, with his desperate cause and his eternal ruin. In spite of your name of Christian, your badge of soldier, and your military oath, you are a servant of Satan, and the Lord will one day cast you out among his open enemies. In God's name, then, no more double dealing. Choose your side! If you wish for despair, and have chosen eternal perdition, then Satan is your master, and you can follow him if you choose. But if Jesus Christ is your king, his service your choice, and his rewards your desire, come to his standard, and flinch no more.

See! the war is raging all around you, in which you must take part, on one side or the other. The banners are flying, the trumpets are sounding, the soldiers of Christ are winning eternal renown and pressing on to battle. Our glorious King is at the head of his chosen band leading the way to victory, which is already waving its wings above the unconquerable standard of salvation. The shouts of conquest are heard in the distance, and the foremost ranks are pressing in as victors through the gates of heaven. Shall we stand here like cowards, hugging the ignominious chains of mortal sin? Far be the thought from every Christian breast! The voice of our Leader is calling us. Forward! then. Onward! let us share in the glorious conflict, that we may share in the triumph, and partake in the everlasting peace that is to follow.

SERMON IX.

THE EPIPHANY.

"They found the Child with Mary his mother."
St. Matt. ii., 2.

(From the Gospel for the Day).

The Feast of the Epiphany, my dear brethren, is as it were a second Christmas. Christmas Day is a feast which all Christians hold in common, whether of Jewish or Gentile blood. If either had more claim than the other, it would seem to belong rather to those who are of Jewish origin; for, "*to you is born this day a Saviour in the City of David*" was the announcement made by the angels to the Jewish shepherds. But this feast of to-day is peculiarly ours. This is the great Gentile-Christian feast.

The motto which we put up over our altar on Christmas eve, and which still hangs there, "*Christus natus est nobis,*" "Christ is born for us," is especially appropriate to-day.

There is, however, still another distinct class of persons to whom this day ought to be especially dear. You, my dear brethren, who had not the greater privilege of belonging to the Holy Catholic Church from your infancy, but whom God in his mercy brought into it in after years, this is your feast. You have an interest in these Gentile converts, your ancestors in the faith, whom the Church commemorates to-day, which they have not who never knew any other creed. What I propose this morning, is,

1. To give you a sketch of the history of to-day's feast; and

2. To show you how these Gentile converts are models of men truly converted to God.

I. History of the Feast.

Whilst angels were telling to the shepherds of Judea, as they kept watch over their flocks on Christmas eve, of the glad tidings of the birth of the Redeemer of the world in Bethlehem, a strange apparition aroused the inhabitants of a great city in the far distant east. They were awakened from their sleep, and the windows, doors, and streets were thronged to look at a bright star, which hung in the sky, just over the city.

You remember, I dare say, what a stir was made in this country and elsewhere, a few years since, by the unexpected appearance of that beautiful comet. How groups were to be seen standing about every evening, both in and out of doors, with telescope or the naked eye, gazing at it, and expressing to one another their wonder and delight. Well, some such feeling as this, mingled with a certain religious awe, must have taken hold of this people of the east on that night. How brilliant! what can it be? what can it mean? how close to us! who will tell us something about it? Exclamations such as these, were heard on all sides, from the lips of rich and poor alike. Now there were men in that kingdom who might naturally be supposed to know something about it, for they had made the science of the stars, in their supposed connection with human action, or astrology, a special branch of study. They were men of education. They were high in civil station too, and filled such offices as magistrate, and governor, and even that of a sort of petty sovereign. They were called Magi. They were in their own country what the Mandarin is in China; what the Brahmin is in India. But how can they know any thing of a star so unusual in its appearance as this? There were two sources through which a certain prophecy connected with the appearance of a star might have reached them.

1. **Fifteen hundred years** before, a prophet or diviner, whatever his office may have been, whose name was **Balaam**, had uttered a most remarkable prophecy. It was as follows: "*I shall see him, but not now; I shall behold him, but not near. A star shall rise out of Jacob, and a sceptre shall spring up from Israel.*" If Balaam was a fellow-countryman of these Magi, as some learned writers have supposed, then they could hardly have been ignorant of this prophecy.

2. One thousand years after that again, the Jews were carried away in captivity to the city of Babylon, and dispersed themselves through that region of country. It is natural

to suppose that in this way their traditions and sacred writings became publicly known. In that case, these men of science could hardly have failed to notice the fact of Balaam's prophecy being found in the Jewish book of Numbers. They would moreover find, in the course of that familiar intercourse which was now established between the people of both nations, that the Jews had always considered this prophecy as having reference to the promised Messias, or future Ruler of their people.

Whatever may be the fact as to their having any information at all, or the particular sources through which it came, or whether their wills were moved directly by inspiration from God, certain it is that these holy kings did recognize in that star their guide to the newly-born king of the Jews. Among the historical records of God's dealing with the Jewish people, they perhaps remembered how He had led them through the wilderness under the guidance of a pillar of fire, and consequently were more willing to trust themselves to a guide of a similar kind.

Difficulties now sprang up on every side. It

was no easy thing to make up their minds to leave their kingdoms (or whatever was the peculiar nature of their charge), in the hands of others, who might usurp their authority in their absence. Travelling over the deserts to the westward was most tedious, and attended with much danger. And after all might not this vision be a delusion? Such were some of the trials their faith had to surmount, and it did surmount them. I will not say more of their journey, than that they were faithful to their guide. They halted when it stood still, they continued their march when it led the way. Here are they now within a short march of the city of Jerusalem. The morning light is breaking, and word is passed to harness the camels, and to fold up the tents. The encampment is alive with joy, at the prospect of the speedy and successful termination of their undertaking, when a cry of distress is heard; "the star!—where is the star? it is gone! what shall we do?" Let us try to conceive what their distress must have been.

You know that in some parts of our country there are great caves underground, into which one can penetrate by paths winding hither and thither to the distance of twenty, thirty, or even forty miles from the entrance; as for example, the great Mammoth cave of Kentucky. Of course, the darkness there is absolute. Perhaps you may remember having seen an account given by one of a party of persons whose only light had gone out on an excursion of this kind. He tried to describe the horror that he and his companions felt when they found themselves in such total darkness, and, unless relieved by persons outside, in the face of certain death. To move, even for a few feet, might, for all they knew, be sudden destruction. To remain where they were was certain death by starvation. Now some such feelings as these must have overwhelmed our travellers from the east when they lost the star. Their guide was gone; they were in a strange and, it might prove, an enemy's land, especially as they had come in search of a rival to him who was sitting on the throne of Judea. What should they do? They determined to enter the city, to go to the king himself and fearlessly demand to know from him " *where is he who is born king of the Jews ; for we have seen his star in the east and have come to worship him?*"

King Herod called in the priests from the temple; the Scriptures were brought, the prophecies were examined; and Bethlehem was found to be the favored spot. "*Thou Bethlehem, the land of Juda, art not the least among the princes of Juda; for out of thee shall come the ruler who shall rule my people Israel.*" They do not stay to be entertained with banquetings, or with what is curious or interesting in this great city, but they resume their journey, when lo! their beautiful guide appears before them once more. Oh! what joy it must have been to them to see it again. I dare say they thought it a hundredfold brighter than before, as they gazed up at it with their cheerful faces. . . . . At last it stops just over a poor shed on a hillside. This the birth-place of the king of the Jews!! Impossible. They look up at the star. There it stands motionless. They dismount with their presents, and pass through the rude entrance. A wonderful light fills the lowly place, and they see a young woman sitting upon some straw on the ground, a beautiful infant on her lap, and one who seems to be her husband, at her side. That same faith which had led them so far, made them bend the knee in adoration. "*They had found the child with Mary his mother.*"

Such, my dear brethren, is the sketch I promised you of this most interesting history of to-day's feast. To me, I must confess it has a peculiar charm and beauty. Now, what holy lesson shall we try to learn from it?

II. THESE MAGI ARE MODELS TO US OF MEN TRULY CONVERTED TO GOD.

1. *In their prompt obedience to his inspirations.* That star was a call from God. He asked a great deal from them. Luxuries, comforts, country, kingdom, home, all must be, for the time at least, abandoned. It would seem so easy for them to have said, as we say now-a-days, 'I can arrange to go in a few months time,—but *at once*, this is quite impossible.' But there stood their bright guide, a rebuke to any such thoughts, and in setting out at once, in obedience to this call from God, these holy men teach us a most wholesome lesson. How often has God not called us, either from some path of sin which we were following, or to a closer union with Himself? At one time He has spoken to us plainly,

by some word in a sermon or book, at another, by some secret fear or inspiration! We answer, "to-morrow, to-morrow," and that morrow never comes. That to-morrow is the devil's light, a very "Will o' the wisp," which leads us on and on to danger and destruction. Oh! let us in future be on the watch for these secret whisperings of grace to our souls, and let us learn to be prompt in corresponding with them.

2. *In their courage.* When these holy men had promptly set about obeying the will of God, their difficulties had only just begun. They would soon have become disheartened but for the supernatural courage that sustained them. Their attendants and servants, not having their Master's faith, magnified every difficulty as it arose. The oppressive heat by day, the cold at night, the length and wearisomeness of the way, the danger of murder and robbery, all these afforded them subjects for continual murmuring. But now, to crown all, the star has disappeared, and they clamor loudly to be allowed to return back in haste to their homes. But no; a courageous faith supported these royal pilgrims, and God rewarded it, by their finding, at last,

THE EPIPHANY. 153

the object of their search, "the Child with Mary his Mother."

How is it, my dear brethren, with us on the way of life? Is it not too common to hear such language as this: 'I have such an unfortunate temper;' or, 'I have such disagreeable neighbors;' or, 'I have such an unmanageable family;' or, 'I am thrown with such reckless companions;' or, 'I have no comfort in my prayers;' and 'There is no use in trying to be good;' 'I would give any thing if I only could be good; I am sure it is the only way to be really happy, but somehow or other I cannot get good.' Oh! poor cowardly souls that we are! Did I not say truly, that in these Magi we should find an occasion of confusion to ourselves, as well as true models of courageous perseverance under difficulties however great or peculiar? Dear brethren, begin again this morning your journey of life, in the spirit of these holy converts. Be faithful to the light that God never fails to give you, through your directors and confessors, through good books and by holy inspirations, and joy and consolation will come all in good time. The only way that will surely, safely, and speedily bring us to our Lord, is the way of the Cross. Surely it is worth the venture, worth the toil, if only we find at last, as we shall, "that Child with Mary his Mother."

3. *In their offerings.* It is a beautiful custom among the nations of the East, that they never go into the presence of their sovereign without some offering. Behold these holy men, as they bow down within the entrance of that poor lodge, and hold out in their hands the gold, the frankincense and the myrrh which they have brought so far, in honor of their newly found Sovereign, the infant king of the Jews! Let us kneel in spirit with them. We have here, our Bethlehem. The infant Jesus is within this little Tabernacle. There, above the altar rail, the still light is burning, which is the silent monitor to our faith, that Jesus is here. The world would have found it hard to adore the infant Saviour, with those three kings, in so lowly a place; and the world finds it too hard now, to kneel with us, in a Catholic church, before the blessed Sacrament. These holy men did not find it hard, nor do we, for they and we have the same blessed gift of faith.

They offer gold—You have none! Oh yes,

you have. Put your ten-penny, five-penny, and three-penny pieces, put your pennies too, into the offertory, with a pure intention, or bestow an alms on the poor outside, in the name of Jesus, and they will be changed into the purest gold. Love is a far more acceptable offering to God than gold. He has no need of your money; for, as the Psalmist says, "The earth is the Lord's, and the fulness thereof." One thing alone you have it in your power to keep from Him, and he deigns to ask you for it. It is your heart. It is your love and your service.

They offer incense—You have none! Oh yes, you have. What does holy king David say? "*O Lord, direct my prayer as incense in thy sight.*" Prayer is the blessed incense that is incessantly streaming up before God. This it is that restrains the arm of his anger, and brings down blessings like showers of rain. There is one prayer above all others which in a special manner is doing this. It is the Holy Mass. Blessed Leonard of Port Maurice asks himself, why it is that God does not nowadays visit nations with such terrible and unmistakable judgments as He did the Jews, and the nations round about them? Then he makes answer to himself, it is because of the all-powerful intercession of the Holy Mass. As that pure and holy sacrifice ascends up like clouds of incense, from ten thousand altars, all over the world, God is disarmed of his anger. A wicked world is spared too, for the sake of what those little tabernacles contain, on the altars of Catholic churches.

Hear mass, then, on a week day, or make a visit of a few minutes to the Blessed Sacrament, and you have the most fragrant incense to offer to God.

They offer myrrh—You have none! Oh yes. Myrrh preserves from corruption. This was among the spices that the holy women brought on Easter morning to embalm our Lord's body. Well, there is something that preserves our souls, as myrrh and spices preserve our bodies. This is self-denial. Self-gratification is the corruption both of soul and body. Look around at the army of drunkards, and seekers of forbidden pleasures, and you will have abundant proof of the corruption of the body, and of the soul too, though not in the awfulness of its corruption, as God sees it.

Well, restrain your tongue; restrain your eye; restrain your appetite; and offer this to God in penance for your sins, in union with that sublime act of self-denial on the Cross, and you will offer to your Saviour as pleasing an offering as these holy Magi.

My brethren, we are all on the road to another, the true Bethlehem. We, too, are going in search of Jesus and Mary. Our Bethlehem is heaven. Our glorious, supernatural, infallible guide, is the Holy Catholic Church. We have met with trials; we shall meet with more. Perhaps, thus far, we have only passed through a sort of preparatory state, which shall enable us to bear up under the real sacrifices that we shall be called upon to make in time to come. Nothing will sustain us under these, but implicit faith in our Guide, and an unshaken fidelity to her. Be loyal to her then. Show your love for God, by your obedience to her. Cling to her side, and she will lead you to that Bethlehem above, where it may be said of you also,—

"They found the Child with Mary his Mother."

SERMON X.

RENUNCIATION.

"And after six days, Jesus taketh unto him Peter and James and John his brother, and bringeth them up into a high mountain apart. And he was transfigured before them. And his face did shine as the sun, and his garments became white as snow."—St. Matt. xvii., 12.

(From the Gospel for the Transfiguration).

A WISE general, in order to excite the ardor of his soldiers, and to render them forgetful of the dangers to which they are exposed, pictures to them on the eve of battle the spoils and glory to be acquired, if they fight bravely. In like manner, our Lord, in order to cheer up and console his disciples, who began to be dismayed at the prospect of that death He was about to suffer, imparted to them a foretaste of the joys of paradise, and a "vision" of the splendor of his divinity. "*He was transfigured before them. And his face did shine as the sun; and his garments became white as snow.*" Peter, as soon as he recovered from his ecstasy of delight, exclaimed: "*Lord, it is good for us to be here.*"

But, to prepare His disciples for this anticipation of heaven, He brought them into a high mountain apart; indicating thereby that such privileges can only be obtained by separation from the world in solitude. This is not only true relative to these high and special favors, but equally true in order to persevere in the practice of a Christian life. Separation from the world is an indispensable duty of a Christian. This truth, so plain in Holy Writ, is nevertheless liable to be misconceived, for which reason we must make the following distinction:

There is a world we are not required as Christians to separate from. There is a world we are under the strictest obligations to separate from.

The condemnation of the world by our Lord and his apostles is too plain and frequent not to have met the eye of any one who has the slightest acquaintance with the New Testament. "*You are from beneath,*" said the Saviour to the Jews, "*I am from above. You are of this world: I am not of this world,*"* "*Love not the world,*" says the beloved disciple and apostle, "*nor the things which are in the world. If any man love the world the charity of the Father is not in him.*"† St. Paul, teaching the Romans, says: "*Be not conformed to the world.*"‡ "*The friendship of the world,*" says St. James, "*is enmity with God,*"§ "*The whole world,*" says St. John, "*is seated in wickedness.*"‖

These declarations of the sacred Scriptures are plain and to the point. To be a disciple of Christ is to have nothing to do with the world. If any further proof were needed of so plain a fact, we may find it in the baptismal service, where the catechumen is engaged by the most solemn promises to turn his back upon the world. But what this world is, that we are so strictly engaged to renounce, is not at first sight so clear.

Is it the visible world, called nature, so full of instruction and rich in beauty, that we are

---

* St. John viii., 23. ‡ Romans xii., 2.
† 1 John ii., 15. § St. James iv., 4.
‖ 1 John v., 19.

to turn our backs upon? Are we called upon in our character as Christians to close our eyes to the flowers, the mountains, the rivers, the glowing sunsets, and the stars of heaven? Are we bound to shut our ears to the murmuring winds, the music of the rivulet, and the songs of the birds? Are we to be counted Christians on the condition only of our shutting out from our senses that beauty, which surrounds us on all hands, of the visible world? What is there profane in nature when Holy Writ assures us that, "*The Lord is holy in all his works.*"* and that "*all things serve Him?*"† The royal prophet David was accustomed to open all the avenues of his soul to the beauty of nature, and, filled with admiration, he seems hardly able to contain his praise of Him by whom all things were made. "*O Lord our Lord, how admirable,*" he exclaims, "*is thy name in the whole earth.*"‡ "*How great are thy works, O Lord! thou hast made all things in wisdom; the earth is filled with thy riches.*"§

Our blessed Saviour himself chose to con-

---

* Psalm cxliv., 13.   ‡ Psalm viii.
† Psalm cxviii., 91.   § Psalm ciii., 24.

vey the great truths of his gospel by illustrations drawn from the visible creation. He calls our attention at one time to "the birds of the air," at another, it is to the golden "harvests," and then it is to "the lilies of the fields." He seems to have looked with an attentive and friendly eye upon the attractions of nature. "*Consider,*" He says, "*the lilies of the fields, how they grow: they labor not, neither do they spin. And yet I say to you that not even Solomon in all his glory, was arrayed like one of these.*"*

Commenting on this passage of Holy Scripture, St. John Chrysostom asks: "Wherefore did God make the lilies so beautiful? That He might display," he answers, "the wisdom and excellency of his power, that from every thing we might learn his glory. For not "*the heavens only declare the glory of God,*"† but the earth too; and this David declared when he said: "*Praise the Lord, ye fruitful trees, and all the cedars.*"‡

It could be no part of the visible creation that the Gospel had in view, when it declared

* St. Matt. vi., 28–29. † Psalm xix., 1.
‡ Psalm cxlviii., 4.

that the friendship of the world is enmity with God; for we hear the same voice speak to us from nature, which speaks to us in divine revelation.

What was it then? Was it the world of art, science, and literature? Have not beauty, knowledge, and genius one and the same fountain source with religion? Whence spring the noble achievements of art, science, and literature, if not from gifts, which like "*every best gift, and every perfect gift, is from above, coming down from the Father of lights.*"* Is not the true aim of art in all its creations to aid religion in bringing men to the contemplation of the first Fair, the first True, and the first Good? Can science find a greater sphere than to show how all things are, and move, and exist in their primal cause, God? Can literature be devoted to more worthy ends than to make those virtues attractive which religion commands? True religion recognizes in art, in science, and in literature, her natural allies, while they in turn find in her bosom loftier and wider spheres to stimulate human exertion. These, then, are not of

* St. James i., 17.

that world which Holy Writ condemns as at enmity with God.

Are we to find the world, which we as Christians are to renounce, in the ties of the family, in relationships and friends, in neighborhood and the common pursuits of life? All these conditions of life our Saviour sanctified either in his own person, or by his express approbation, or by his presence. The basis of all these relations of human life is that of marriage, and this natural tie, He not only sanctioned, but raised it up to a holy sacrament of his religion. It is a false idea of the Christian religion, and one which is most injurious, to imagine that it requires of us to stifle all natural affections, and to escape from society, in order to lead a Christian life. It teaches that the way of salvation, and the high roads to sanctity, are chiefly through the fulfilment of the common duties of every day life. "*For God created all things*" says Holy Writ, "*that they might be: and he made the nations of the earth for health: and there is no poison of destruction in them, nor kingdom of hell upon earth.*"* The world

* Wisdom i., 14.

made up of human relationships and the common pursuits of life, called society, is not at enmity with God. Nature art, science, human society, are not opposed to Christianity, nor contrary to Christian perfection. Many Christians have become great saints surrounded only by the scenery of nature; others while cultivating the arts and sciences; others again have reached an eminent degree of perfection while fulfilling their common every day duties. For the visible creation is good, and there is nothing in man's nature incompatible with the absolute perfections of God, as is proved in the fact that our Saviour was in all respects in his humanity a man, and at the same time truly God. "*All things,*" says Holy Scripture, "*co-operate for good to those who love God.*" The true Christian Church incorporates and consecrates nature and art in her worship—she appeals to the whole nature of every man, and opens a way to heaven for men of all classes, and in every condition of society.

The task was left to the sects which sprung from the religious revolution of the sixteenth century, to exclude nature and art from Christian worship, to divorce faith and science, to degrade the sacrament of matrimony to a mere civil contract, and to teach men that they were wholly depraved. The authors of this revolution in Christianity, seemed to take delight in parcelling the realm of Christian truth into wrangling creeds, and in rendering Christian worship rigid, gloomy and repulsive. And in this they found freedom, progress, and the light of the pure gospel!

How narrow and grovelling are the minds which never rise to the contemplation of that unity which reconciles all truths, all beauties, and all goodness! Will that day ever dawn when Christianity will find a people sufficiently great to grant to its divine truths fair play with their intelligence, and a full sway to her influence over their whole lives?—when men of genius, of science and of learning will understand that the true end of all knowing, all loving and all doing is the same as that of religion, to render the souls of men more like their Creator, and to aid others in this divine work?

Where then is the world which, as Christians, we are called upon to separate from? There is a world which God made for the use of man. He made it good, and good it remains while rightly used. There is another world which man has made, and it is framed out of the abuse of the creatures of God's world.

The whole difficulty lies in the fact that men generally do not consider the things of creation rightly, or use them properly; and the great world around us consists in the main of those who thus misunderstand God's world, and live by the abuse and perversion of it, led on by their inordinate desires. This is "the world seated in wickedness," on which we must turn our backs, for to be a friend of it, is to be an enemy of God. A few illustrations will make this point plain.

How few there are who look upon nature in that light in which she was intended to be seen by her Creator. Seen in this light, the whole visible world of nature raises up our thoughts and affection to our common Creator. For nature has ever been true and loyal to her Author. The Psalmist only gives expression to the natural and spontaneous impulses of the soul when in beholding the visible world, he exclaims: " *O Lord, our Lord, how admirable is thy name in the whole earth.*" How few in looking upon nature, raise up their thoughts to nature's God. They do not go beyond, but stop with what they see. To them, nature is the highest and most complete expression of strength, beauty, and truth. Nature is fair, but how much fairer is He who made nature what she is! They forget the King in their blind admiration of his vestments. They become the servants and slaves of nature, instead of being her master and high-priest. Their worship of nature excludes her Creator and Lord, and they become like the heathen idolaters of whom the Apostle speaks: "*They worshipped the creature rather than the Creator, who is blessed for ever.*"*

What do we find for the most part in the world of art? Do we see artists who are conscious of the great purposes of their noble vocation? Do they aim by the creations of their genius to raise less gifted minds to gaze upon the archetype of all beauty, truth, and goodness? Do they strive so to embody what is noblest and best in man's nature as to captivate his imagination, and enkindle an enthusiasm for its imitation? There are a few such; a few

* Rom. i., 25.

who are men, no less than artists, and who regard their vocation as something akin to what is sacred, and would look upon it as desecration to employ their gifts in such way as to lead men aside from the realization of the great end of their existence. But the many study to clothe with forms of borrowed beauty the expressions which spring from the lowest passions of their nature. The lessons which their productions teach, were they interpreted and expressed in words, would shock the unvitiated feelings of the heart, causing the innocent cheek to blush with shame. Quoting with sophistical blindness the text, "*To the pure all things are pure*," they imagine they are justified in violating every rule of Christian decency, every feeling of modesty, and every maxim of morality. Under the pretext of being true to nature, they misrepresent nature, by presenting what is lowest in man, and that in its exaggerated and depraved developments, and thereby add excitement to his already inordinate appetites and aid powerfully to his further degradation. Art, instead of being an angel pointing with its fore-finger to heaven, showing man the way to his destiny, and aiding him to its attainment, is turned into a Siren, enticing men to sin and destruction.

In the world of science and literature, the same thing takes place. It would appear that the aim of most men devoted to science is, in a great measure, to undermine the basis of religious conviction in the soul, instead of adding to its strength and support. What is more reasonable than to suppose that the sentiments of religion should increase in proportion to the acquisition of the knowledge of truth, for the end of all knowledge of truth is God. And yet, if you select from almost any branch of science, those who are pre-eminent, you will, in all probability, find that those who believe in Christianity and practise its precepts, are in the minority, a very small minority. What a strange perversion of the gift of intelligence to study the works of creation, in order to overturn the Revelation of the Creator!

Popular literature is of the same stamp. It would be high praise to say of a popular author that his writings contain nothing contrary to morals or religion. It would seem to be the aim of some to substitute vice for virtue, and so to cloak passion with the garb of innocence as to make obedience to them an act of religion. Familiarity with our popular literature would be a sad preparation for the reception of religious impressions, or for the practice of virtue. Briefly, in art, in science, and literature, there reigns for the greater part, an indifference to Christianity, the spirit of paganism, and a practical atheism.

Let us now look about ourselves in society. Here is a man possessed with the desire for distinction and places of honor. His thoughts by day, and his dreams at night, are set upon them. He is a lawyer, and aims at being at the head of the bar, or at becoming a judge. He is a politician, he seeks to be an alderman, or a state senator, or a congressman. He knows not but one day he may be the president of the United States. Does he seek these by legitimate means? Not at all. To gain popularity he sacrifices all self-respect, and bribery is connived at to obtain votes. If his religion is likely to aid his efforts, he *uses* it; you will find him in church, and he gives liberally about election times to its charitable institutions. Should his religion stand in his way, he ceases to practice its duties. Should it serve his purpose, he becomes a free-mason, or an odd-fellow, or a member of some other secret society.

Another is driven on by an inordinate desire for riches. Not content with the rewards of an honest trade, or a respectable business, he must make money easier and faster. He starts a saloon or a liquor store, and to conceal the low and disgraceful character of his traffic, he places on his house a sign in large letters, "Bonded Warehouse," "Rectifying Distillery," "Importer of Foreign Liquors," or some other like falsehood. His foreign and domestic wines and liquors, are made of bad spirits, some coloring matter and essences, with fusil oil; and these he deals out for genuine, making from two to three hundred per cent. profit. Under the plea of providing for a family, and it may be that he has neither chick nor child, he opens in the city several such—Rectifying Distilleries!! What does this man care about the scandal which he is the occasion of to his religion, or the poverty and wretchedness he spreads abroad in his neighborhood, or the number of souls which he sends to an untimely and unprepared grave, caused by his poisonous stuffs, so that he gain wealth without effort and rapidly.

Another, a young man who is bent upon seeking pleasure. He frequents low theatres, ball-rooms, and bar-rooms. He meets companions, he gambles, and occasionally he puts his hand in the till of his employer's drawer, or he forges his paper. The effects of late hours, intoxication and debauchery, by and by, show themselves on his face, a faint picture of the corruption which these vices have produced in his heart. He ends his life as an uncurable in a public hospital; or detected, he spends his time and dies in a penitentiary.

Here is a girl whose mind and imagination are filled with parties of pleasure, and forbidden friendships, gathered for the most part from reading popular literature and infectious novels. Her prayers are forgotten, the sacraments neglected, and she dreams of amusements and romantic attachments. Dress, tone of voice, every step and movement of her person betray the inordinate passions which have taken possession, and reign now in her bosom. To fill up the sketch, all that is now needed is time and opportunity, to complete her ruin, and make her a public shame.

From these illustrations it is easily seen which world it is that, as followers of Christ, we are to separate from. It is this world fabricated of error, of the abuse of created things, and engendered of inordinate desires. This is the world of which the Apostle speaks when he says: "*Love not the world, nor the things which are in the world. If any man love the world the charity of the Father is not in him: for all that is in the world, is the concupiscence of the flesh, the concupiscence of the eyes, and the pride of life, which is not of the Father but of the world.*"*

There is then a world which is formed of the things which God has made, and the right use of these things by us; and this is an innocent and righteous world, of which it is said: "*God was in Christ, reconciling the world to himself.*"† There is a world which is made up of error, and the abuse men make of created things; and this is the wicked and ungodly world condemned in Holy Scripture. On the one let us look with interest and delight,

* 1 John ii., 15. † 2 Cor. v., 9.

and from the other let us separate and stand far apart, as did our blessed Lord and his Saints, giving heed to the advice of St. Augustine: "Let the spirit of God be in thee," he says, "that thou mayest see that all these created things are good; but woe to thee if thou love the things made, and forsake the Maker of them! Fair are they to thee; but how much fairer He that formed them!"

SERMON XI.

THE AFFLICTIONS OF THE JUST.

"Blessed are you, when men shall revile you, and persecute you, and shall say all manner of evil against you, for my sake. Rejoice, and be exceeding glad, because your reward is very great in heaven; for so they persecuted the Prophets that were before you."—St. Matt. v., 11, 12.

(From the Gospel for All Saints' Day.)

I AM about to preach you an old sermon this morning; but I doubt not, my dear friends, you will find it all the better for being old, and quite appropriate, moreover, to this day's feast, for it will carry us back to the earlier ages of Christianity, when living saints were more abundant than now.

In a vast desert of Palestine, which lay near the boundaries of Arabia, there dwelt, during the fourth century of the Christian era, a number of devout hermits, who, after a life of great innocence and saintly virtue, were cruelly massacred by the Saracens. Some of their brethren, deeply afflicted and scandalized by this outrage, began to ask themselves, how it was possible that God should permit such holy men to perish by the hand of these wicked infidels. In their perplexity, they deputed several of their number to visit and consult an aged Egyptian hermit who, on account of the great veneration in which he was held, and the number of disciples gathered around him, was called the Abba, or Abbot Theodore. These came to him with their sad story, and besought him to explain why God should permit such holy men to perish so miserably, and how he could consent to the triumph of these cruel barbarians over his saints.

I invite your particular attention, my brethren, to his answer; for perhaps you have asked similar questions yourselves. In the various wars in which nations have engaged, and even in those where the interests of religion seemed most involved, we do not see that victory has always perched upon those banners which the prayers of God's people have blessed. So it has been throughout the history of the Church, and especially during the past three centuries. Who can recount the calamities which from year to year have fallen upon the children of the faith? The soul grows sick to read of kingdoms wrested by violence into schism and heresy, the burnings of monasteries and convents, or their confiscation to the state, the persecution of the Catholic clergy, the oppression of the laity. And especially when we turn our thoughts to Ireland, poor, faithful, downtrodden Ireland—is it not wonderful that every thing seems to turn out to her disadvantage, and to the prosperity of her oppressors? Have you not sometimes been tempted to exclaim: "Has God forgotten Ireland? Has she clung to her faith so long in vain, amid poverty, oppression and bloodshed? Has heaven no favors for her? Why does not God give victory always to the just cause?" Or, perhaps, you have noticed in your own neighborhood, how often the most faithful servants of God have been visited by heavy afflictions, long sickness, loss of property, death of children and other dear friends, while others, destitute of faith, piety, and of all virtuous principle, seem to prosper on every hand. And perhaps, seeing this, the thought arises in your mind: "Does not God take notice of these things? Has He no chastisement for the wicked, no sympathy for the good? Why does He not take part with his own, and make them prosper most?" All these murmurings are like those of the good anchorites who visited Abbot Theodore, and his answer to their questions will answer yours.

(*Prelude of Abbot Theodore.*)—"These questions, my brethren," said he, "only astonish those who, having little faith and little light, think that the saints ought to receive their recompense in this life, while God reserves it for them in the other. But we have far different thoughts. If our hopes in Christ were only for the present life, we should be, as St. Paul tells us, the most miserable among men, having no recompense in this world, and losing heaven also by our want of faith. We ought to guard our minds against this error, for it would leave us without hope or courage in the moment of temptation, fill us with distrust of God, and so bring us into sin, and to our ruin." After this short prelude, he goes on to show that God neither sends nor permits any real evil to those that love Him, but that, on the contrary, all things contribute to the welfare of the just. And this is his argument:

I. God neither sends nor permits any real evil, &c.

"Every thing in this world," said the good abbot, "is either good, or bad, or indifferent. There is nothing really good but virtue, which conducts us to God. There is nothing really bad but sin, which separates us from God. Indifferent things are such as hold a middle place between good and evil, and may pass into one or the other, according to the disposition of him that uses them. Such are riches, honor, health, beauty, life, death, sickness, poverty, injuries, insults, &c."

"This distinction laid, let us see whether God has ever sent any real evil to his saints, or permitted any one to do them a real injury. That is something that we shall never be able to make out. For no one is able to make a man fall into sin, who is unwilling and resists, but only those who consent to it, and give admittance to it, by the effeminacy of their hearts, and the depravity of their will. The demon employed every possible artifice against holy Job to make him murmur against God; but in spite of all the afflictions which he heaped upon him, body and soul, he could not provoke him so far as to sin even with his lips, and thus fall into the only real evil he had to fear. We must not think, therefore, that the ill turns which our enemies or other persons sometimes do us are really evils, but they belong rather to the class of indifferent things. To be sure, they may think to have done us harm, and rejoice at it; but the harm does not depend upon what they may think, so long as we do not count it for such. For example: a good man is put to death, without any just cause or provocation. Now, we must not suppose that any thing really evil in itself has happened to him, but simply something which is either good or evil, according to circumstances. For, in truth, death, which is commonly counted to be an evil, comes with a blessing to the just man, for it delivers him from all the afflictions of this life. Thus death is no harm to him; and although the malice of his enemies anticipates the order of nature by leading him to a sudden death, the good man thereby only pays a little sooner a debt which he had to pay in any case, and he goes to receive an eternal crown, as the reward of his sufferings and death."

Upon this, one of the party named Germanus, raised a difficulty. "In that case," said he, "we should have no reason to blame the murderer, since he does no harm to the one he kills, but only speeds him the sooner on to his salvation."

"We are speaking of things as they are in themselves," said Abbot Theodore, "and not of the intention of those who do them. The patience and virtue of the just man in his sufferings and death, is a crown to himself, but no justification of his persecutor. The latter will be punished for his cruelty, and for the evil which he intended to do, while the good man has in reality suffered no harm, but by his patience has changed into a blessing the evil which was devised against him. For example: the wonderful patience of Job was of no service to Satan, but it was of inestimable value to Job himself, who endured his trials with so much courage and resignation. So Judas is none the less subjected to eternal torments, because his treason contributed to the salvation of men; for in the eye of divine justice, an action is not so much to be judged by its results, as by the intention of the person who did it."

These high and holy maxims of Christian philosophy being thus firmly established, our good hermit, growing warm with his subject, begins to rise to still loftier and more beautiful conceptions, like a bee coming out from its search in the flower, and shaking the golden pollen from its wings.

II. ALL THINGS CONTRIBUTE TO THE WELFARE OF THE JUST.

"We say of some men that they are born to good luck, and that every thing they put their hands to turns out well. We deceive ourselves when we say this; it is only true of the Saints, and in a spiritual sense. '*We know,*' says St. Paul, '*that all things work together for good to them that love God.*'* Wonderful truth! Beautiful truth! And the Prophet David says the same thing of every man whose will is in the Law of God: '*All, what-*

* Rom. viii., 28.

soever he shall do, shall prosper.'* Now, when the Apostle says that '*all things work together for good,*' he means not only prosperity, but also what is called adversity. And why? Why, because those who truly and perfectly love God remain unchanged in all the vicissitudes of life. They have but one end in view —eternal life, and only one means to attain to it, namely, to do the will of God. This they can do in all weathers, in rain or sunshine. Indeed, like the stormy petrel, they gather most in stormy weather. For what reflecting Christian does not know the sweet uses of adversity, which, by severing the hopes that bound us to the earth, and opening our eyes to the fact that we are but pilgrims here, with a right of passage only, teach us to fix our hopes on heaven alone, and labor to build up our fortunes there? The great Apostle, who himself had passed through the various paths of adversity, teaches us how to turn all the vicissitudes of life, both its joys and sorrows, into golden occasions of merit, fighting our way onward to heaven, as he says, '*with the strength which God gives us, by the arms of*

* Ps. i., 3.

justice, on the right hand and on the left;" that is, as he goes on to explain, '*through honor and dishonor, through infamy and good name, as dying and behold we live, as sorrowful and yet always rejoicing, as having nothing and yet possessing all things.*'*

"All therefore, that passes for prosperity, and is consequently *on the right hand*, such as glory, and good reputation, and success in temporal affairs, and all that passes for adversity, and thus, according to the language of St. Paul, is *on the left hand*, such as disgrace and evil report, and temporal disappointment;—all to the perfect Christian serve alike for arms of justice, holy weapons to win his crown with, because he receives every thing that comes with the same great heart, and allows himself to be cast down by nothing. And therefore the Prophet says of him: '*The holy man continues in wisdom like the sun.*'† But for those who change every moment, and show different humors and different dispositions of heart, according to the different chances and changes of life—let them listen to these words of the same Prophet, which were spoken for their

* 2 Cor. vi. † Ecclus. xxvii. 12.

especial benefit: '*The fool changes like the moon.*'* And, therefore, every thing turns to evil for them, according to the proverb: '*Every thing to the foolish man is contrary,*'† because he does not improve in prosperity, nor correct his ways in adversity. It will not do for the Christian to be like wax, which takes any form that may be impressed upon it; but like a diamond seal, he should keep unchangeably the form impressed upon his heart by the hand of God, showing no change in the different events of life.

"In Holy Scripture‡ we read of one Aod, a great warrior, and a leader of the Israelites, who was what is called an *ambidexter*, that is, he could use the left hand as well as the right. This man," said Abbot Theodore, "is a type of the perfect Christian, who is always an ambidexter, making use of both prosperity and adversity to advance the salvation of his soul, and increase his merits, fighting the good fight of faith, '*with the arms of justice, on the right hand and on the left.*' It is the duty of us all to exercise ourselves in the use of this holy

---

* Ecclus. xxvii., 12. † Prov. xiv. 7. So in the lxx.
‡ Judges ii.

armor, that we may, like Aod, be dexterous warriors, able to carry our swords in either hand, and meet our foes on whatever side they may advance, temperate in prosperity, patient in adversity, never fainting, always rejoicing, seeking for nothing, hoping for nothing, knowing nothing in this world but "Jesus Christ and Him crucified," and thus, by this blessed alchemy of the Saints, turning all things into gold.

"You see, therefore, my dear friends," so concluded the good hermit, "that we have no occasion to deplore the death of these saintly solitaries, as if they had suffered some great misfortune, or as if their enemies had triumphed over them; and still less have we any right to complain of God, as if He had forsaken or forgotten his own. On the contrary, they have gone to their rest, like the laboring man at night-fall; they have been shaken from the tree where they grew, like ripe figs in the harvest time, and their Divine Master has gathered them in. Their death was cruel and miserable in the eyes of man, but precious in the sight of God, for so the Psalmist tells us: '*Precious in the sight of God is the death of his Saints.*'*

* Psalm cxv., 15.

Do not believe that, even if it were left to their choice, they would wish to come back again to this world, to live longer in it, nor would they choose any other death than that by which they have quitted it. Indeed there was little room for choice in the matter, since, as the Apostle says, *'for them to live was Christ and to die was gain,'** it being the privilege of the Saints to prosper in all that befalls them."

See! my dear brethren, it is not I that have been speaking to you, but an ancient Father of the desert. I have preached to you an old sermon, and well nigh word for word as it was spoken fifteen hundred years ago in the Egyptian wilderness. I have done so purposely, in order that you may take notice that the Christians of those early times were subject to disasters and afflictions as you are now, and tried by the same temptations. You see also what kind of consolation they found in their religion, what kind of counsel they received from their spiritual advisers, and how they turned their sorrows and adversities to good account. Their time of trial was over long ago; and now they are happy. No doubt, they look

* Phil. i., 21.

back with pleasure upon those very sorrows, as belonging to the sweetest and holiest days of their pilgrimage on earth—days of patient resignation, and childlike trust, and Christian courage — days when they wept much, but prayed all the more—days when the current of earthly joys was at its lowest ebb-tide, but the waters of heavenly grace were at their fullest flood-tide, and therefore, days of golden gain. Oh! let it be so with you, my brethren, in your afflictions! What would you have? The Christians of other ages have journeyed on cheerfully toward heaven bearing their cross. Would you ride thither at your ease? Would you wear your crown without winning it? Would you be saved by the sufferings of Christ, and refuse to take your share of suffering? No! arm yourselves with Christian fortitude. Meet adversities patiently, manfully, trustfully, as these good Christians did of old. Be like them in the trials of this world, and then, like them too in the recompense of the other, "*your sorrows shall be turned into joy,*" and your joy will be all the greater for the sorrows you have endured.

SERMON XII.

FALSE MAXIMS.

"Lord, that I may see."—St. Luke xviii., 41.

(From the Gospel for Quinquagesima Sunday.)

BLINDNESS is a very common thing, if we may judge by the many false maxims afloat. We find them everywhere and in every thing, in politics, in business, in the government of children, in religion. Wherever they are, they are pernicious and destructive. In business they lead to bankruptcy and ruin; in politics to disunion, revolution and anarchy; in the government of families to dissipation and worthlessness. But of all false maxims, the most pernicious and destructive are those relating to religion: because they involve the loss of the soul, of all our interests, hopes, and happiness in one great ruin.

There are many such. One will say: "It's no matter what a man's faith may be. All religions are alike, they are different roads that lead to the same end. Let a man only act right, and he can throw all creeds overboard; whether Jew, Turk, Heathen, Protestant or Catholic, it makes no difference." A man who speaks thus is no Catholic, nor is he ever like to be. He has put out the light of Jesus Christ, who holds up to us "one faith, one Lord, one baptism," and gropes along to his ruin in a darkness of his own creation. But I don't mean to speak of such. I would rather speak of the false maxims of certain Catholics by which they persuade themselves that all will be right, though the Lord and Savior says that all is wrong, and so rush blindly to their ruin.

One of the first of these maxims is this: *Because I'm a Catholic I shall be sure to get to heaven.* Where did such a notion come from? You are sure of heaven only on condition of behaving yourself as you ought. If you have a ticket on the cars and misbehave, you are put off at the first station; so whatever rights you have to heaven in virtue of being a Catholic are forfeited when you cease to live as a Catholic ought to live. If you sin, your being a Catholic won't hinder you from losing all the privileges of your baptism. Where did you get the notion that it's enough to be a Catholic without being a practical one? Was it from the Church of God? The very first word addressed you by her, was in your baptism, when you were asked: "What dost thou ask of the Church of God?" The answer was: "Faith." "What does faith bring thee to?" was the next question. The reply was: "Eternal life." Then spoke out the Church right solemnly: "If thou wilt enter into life *keep the commandments.*" Keeping the commandments is here the plain condition for obtaining eternal life, and nothing else. That's what the Lord himself said to the young man who asked the question: "What shall I do that I may have everlasting life?" His reply was in the very same words: "*Keep the commandments.*"* To whom is that addressed? To Catholics. Who says it? The God of

* St. Matt. xix., 16, 17.

heaven and earth. Do you believe Him? If you do, you must give up the idea of being saved merely because you are a Catholic, but expect salvation by being a good one, and keeping the commandments. What's more, the Divine Scriptures expressly state that it is not enough to profess the faith without good works. "*Know ye not that the unjust shall not possess the kingdom of God. Be not deceived: neither fornicators, nor adulterers, nor idolaters, nor the effeminate, nor thieves, nor the covetous, nor drunkards, shall possess the kingdom of God.*"* Who are addressed? Heathens? No; they are Catholics; the Corinthians who had been baptized and received the sacraments. Under what figure is the Church of God represented in Scripture? As a net that contains fish both good and bad. Yes, they are not all good fish that are in the net; there are bad ones. What is said of these bad ones? That at the last day they shall be sorted out and given to the fire. The Church is compared to a field sown with good grain and overrun with tares. Are the tares rooted up in this world? No, they grow together with

---

* 1 Cor. vi., 9, 10.

the wheat until the harvest; that is, until the judgment at the end of the world: then comes the division, and the burning of the tares. Listen to the explanation of the Lord: "*So shall it be at the end of the world. The Angels shall go out and shall separate the wicked from among the just, and shall cast them into the furnace of fire; there shall be weeping and gnashing of teeth.*"* If you are acting on any such maxim you have blinded yourself, you have put out the light of the Gospel of Jesus Christ, and walk in a way of your own devising, to your eternal destruction.

Another false principle of a great many is this: *Because they don't lead what they call very bad lives, they cannot, as they imagine, be among the damned:* In other words, they don't and won't believe that one mortal sin is the death of the soul. Where did this notion come from? From the Church? I would like to know where. What Apostles, Doctors of the Church, Pontiffs, Priests, or Laymen, that ever wrote on the matter, ever broached such an idea? For eighteen hundred long

* St. Matt. xiii., 49.

years the Church, we may say, has done nothing else but repeat over and over that one mortal sin will damn the soul. Did any Priest ever preach to the contrary? I never heard one do so; I never heard of one who had done so. And yet, Catholic people do sometimes get this folly into their minds. An old man, quite a respectable one too, came to me not long ago: "Father, I have a temptation on a point of faith." "What is it?" "I can't believe that one mortal sin will damn the soul. I heard the Missionary say so in his sermon, but I didn't believe him. I think I have heard the contrary from other Priests." I said to him: "My friend, I cannot believe you ever did. It's a notion you've picked up from another quarter." Why, what do we mean when we speak of mortal sin? The very word mortal means deadly. Don't you see, the very definition of mortal sin, is a sin that grievously offends God and brings with it the death of the soul? It is deliberately rejecting God with your eyes wide open. Once is enough. Spit in a man's face once, you need not do it a second time. Play the hypocrite with him once, he won't trust you again. Renounce his friendship once, and friendship is over. Your friend will forgive you many little offences, but trample once on some right, on some feeling which he holds dear and sacred, and once is enough. How many times must you spit in God's face, play the hypocrite with Him, turn your back on Him, trample on His most sacred commandments, before you expect Him to be angry? One mortal sin is enough because it is mortal." Many don't and won't believe this. Hear what they say: "I'm a good one to attend mass. I don't miss it of my own fault more than five or six times a year." "Do you ever get drunk?" "Oh, not a great deal, only a reasonable share, now and again, a few times in the course of the year;" and so on of other things. The devil has blinded them. They are travelling along with the great crowd, singing and laughing, down the broad road that leads to the pit of hell. Listen to what the Scriptures say: "*Be converted and do penance for all your iniquities, and iniquity shall not be your ruin. Cast away from you all your transgressions by which you have transgressed, and make to yourself a new heart, and a new spirit; for why will you die,*

*O house of Israel."** That's it. "All" is the word. Nothing short of this will save from ruin.

Another false maxim: *That we shall be saved by the sacraments, no matter how we receive them.* A great many have evidently some such principle lurking in their minds. The way they make confession shows it. The only idea with them seems to be to wipe off old scores and to be at more liberty to begin afresh. The load of sin gets heavy; it begins to press upon the conscience; it makes one uneasy. What's to be done to get rid of it? Pitch it off upon the Priest's back. Then he will become responsible; they need give themselves no farther trouble about it. They have brought the same load of mortal sin now for many years, perhaps every half-year, and, what's more, they really expect to do the same until their death. Some come concealing their sins time and again. If an absolution can be got out of the Priest, it makes no matter how. It is the absolution they want; all the same to them whether God sanctions it or not. So when the Priest refuses, seeing that they are not prepared, they beg for it. "Oh

---
* Ezechiel xviii., 30, 31.

Father, do give me the absolution!" "You are not fit for it." "Oh, but you can give it if you please," they say. Sometimes they threaten, "If I'm not absolved, I won't come again." Sometimes they plead occupation: "If I go away without absolution, I cannot come again without great inconvenience;" as if their convenience should entitle them to absolution, without penitence, and the purpose of amendment.

This is indeed taking out of the sacraments all their life and spirit, and reducing them to a mere form. This is what our Lord called the religion of the Scribes and Pharisees, who made clean the outside of the platter, but left the inside greasy and filthy. These go through the form of confession, merely keeping up an outside appearance of piety, but their hearts are full of rottenness and filth. Does the Church teach any such thing? No, far from it. She teaches that the indispensable condition of forgiveness is a true, heartfelt sorrow for every mortal sin, with a firm, unflinching determination to avoid every such sin for the rest of one's life. She is the *Holy* Catholic Church, and her teaching is as pure as the sunlight on this point; it is clearly laid down in all her catechisms and instructions, so that no one need make any mistake about it. Nevertheless the Lord foresaw that many would blind themselves in spite of all this. He represents them standing at the judgment and saying: "*Lord, have we not eaten and drunk at thy table?*"* Yes, we received the sacraments; certainly there can't be any mistake, it must be all right. What is the answer? "*Depart from me, workers of iniquity, I know not whence ye are.*"† Sacraments received wrongfully work out, not the salvation, but the damnation of the soul. So St. Paul speaks of those who, through their sins, did not discern the Lord's body, being weak and sickly —speaks also of eating and drinking judgment to one's self.

If this last is a false and fatal error, how much more horrible is it when it assumes a new shape and comes out in this form: *Oh, I will live as I please, and the last sacraments will make it all right. I'll send for the priest before I die.* Judas when finishing his act of perfidy, kissed the Saviour whom he had deliber-

* St. Luke xiii., 26. † St. Luke xiii., 27.

ately and **wantonly betrayed.** So these desert and betray Christ and his holy religion, and then go to make it up with a last kiss; a kiss full of hypocrisy and only given through a dire necessity that presses them. Is any hope held out in Scripture for the victims of such delusions? *"If ye live according to the flesh ye shall die."** *"What a man soweth that shall he reap."*† *"Ye shall cry unto me Lord, but the Lord will not hear you."* *"Ye shall seek me and ye shall not find me; ye shall die in your sins."*‡ Small comfort this to those who are cheating themselves with the idea of sending for the priest, and receiving the sacraments on their death-beds. Priests and sacraments, if they do receive them (which is a thing extremely doubtful), will do no good without contrition, and who will answer for the contrition of one who has persisted in outraging God through a whole life, and who, now that death stares him in the face, and in the midst of pain and fever and stupor, must set the accounts of conscience in order. The whole demeanor of such persons shows, **only too frequently,** how little they realize **their condition,** and what a

---

* Rom. viii., 13. † Gal. vi., 7. ‡ St. John viii., 21.

wretched reliance death-bed repentance is, for the salvation of the soul.

Such are some of the false maxims that put out the eyes of the soul. Whence do they spring? From an evil and perverse heart. A man given up to sin must justify himself in some way or other. He therefore makes light of sin—seeks to persuade himself that its consequences are not so dreadful—that after all, when it comes to the very point, God will not allow these consequences to fall upon him. They say a drowning man will catch at a straw. So these persons, though they know the truth, catch at every straw that holds out the least prospect of safety—every flimsy pretense that holds out encouragement for a life of sin; every false maxim that holds out a ground of hope. They call such things up on every occasion to fortify their own minds. They repeat them over to their friends, as if by hearing them a number of times they might seem to have more foundation in them. They like to hear others say such things; it gives them a wonderful encouragement to go on. So the blind lead the blind. At last this false reasoning gets to be so habitual that they fall back upon it whenever conscience begins to speak to their hearts. As to turning to God and quitting sin, that they won't think of even for a moment; so, in the words of Scripture, "*a strong delusion is sent upon them to believe a lie.*" It is sent upon them, in the sense that they have drawn it on themselves. To be sure, they don't really believe it, but they wish to believe it, try to believe it, and fancy that they do believe it. Indeed, in practice they may be said to believe, inasmuch as they have made up their minds to act upon it. What a miserable state to be in is this! Self-satisfied and self-blindfolded, to be drifting down into hell, in a dream of careless and stupid indifference! The poor blind man cried out with all his might, "*Lord! that I may see!*" The loss of bodily sight is indeed a great calamity, a thing to be keenly felt. The bare possibility of being restored to sight, should be enough to make one cry out, with his whole soul, 'Lord, Lord, that I may receive my sight!' How much more deplorable when the eyes of the soul are put out! How much more occasion to cry out in agony of spirit to Jesus the true light, that enlightens every man that cometh into the world—'Lord! that I may see! that I may understand the things that belong to my peace; that I may arouse from my stupidity, throw away all false delusions, and square myself by the maxims of the Gospel, opening my eyes to those eternal truths revealed by a God who can neither deceive nor be deceived!'

Oh sinner! oh careless, indifferent Christian! if you have the least desire to make your hope of heaven a sure hope, one that shall not be confounded, cry with the blind man to Jesus, "*Lord, that I may see!*" Cry aloud, repeat that cry, until Jesus shall turn to you, and grant your request. Show that you are in earnest by taking the means to get your soul enlightened. Go and hear the word of God preached on the Sundays. Don't do as so many do, that go to Low Mass, early, and hear no sermon from one month to another. Make a practice to go to High Mass, where Jesus Christ, in the person of his priest, stands on purpose to give you light. How can you expect light when you close your eyes? How will the truths of the Gospel reach your heart and make an impression there, if you never listen to them? Preaching is the appointed means of receiving the truth. "*Faith cometh by hearing!*" says the Holy Ghost.* Imitate the blind man. He found out where Jesus was expected to come by; he went there. Do likewise. Go where Jesus is, to the Church; cry to Him; listen to Him; when He speaks through his holy Gospels; read them, and hear them explained by the living voice of his representative the Priest. Then you will have light; you will have it abundantly, to your great joy and consolation.

The promise is sure; there can be no failure. "*If any of you lack wisdom let him ask of God, who giveth to all abundantly and upbraideth not, and it shall be given him.*† Ask for it, and you shall receive it. What is it? The light that shall direct our feet in the way of peace, and carry us through safely to the light of glory in heaven. The light of Christ, "*in which the Priest from on high hath visited us, to enlighten them that sit in darkness and in the shadow of death: to direct our feet in the way of peace.*"‡

* Rom. x., 17.   † St. James i., 5.
‡ St. Luke i., 78.

SERMON XIII.

MARY'S DESTINY A TYPE OF OURS.

"Mary hath chosen the best part, which shall not be taken away from her."—St. Luke x., 42.

(From the Gospel for the Assumption.)

To-day is the Assumption of the Blessed Virgin Mary. To-day she entered into the enjoyment of heaven. The trials and troubles of life are over. The time of banishment is ended. She closes her eyes on this world and opens them to the vision of God. She is exalted to-day above the choirs of angels to the heavenly kingdom, and takes her seat at the right hand of her Son. I do not mean to attempt any description of her glory in heaven. I am sure whatever I could say would fall far short, not only of the reality, but of your own glowing thoughts about her. Who is there that needs to be told that the Blessed Virgin is splendid in sanctity, dazzling in beauty, and exalted in power? But, my brethren, it is possible to contemplate the Blessed Virgin in such a way as to put her at too great a distance from us. It is possible to conceive of her glory in heaven as flowing entirely from her dignity as Mother of God, and therefore to suppose it altogether unattainable by us; and as a consequence of this, to regard her with feelings full of admiration indeed, but almost as deficient in sympathy as if she were of another nature from us. Now this is to rob ourselves of so ennobling and encouraging a part of our privilege as Christians, and at the same time to take away from our devotion to the Blessed Virgin an element so useful and important, that I have determined, on this her glorious Feast, to remind you that our destiny and the destiny of Mary are substantially the same.

And the first proof I offer of this is, that the glory of the Blessed Virgin in heaven is *not* owing to her character as Mother of God, but to her correspondence to grace—to her good works—to her love of God—in a word, to her fidelity as a Christian. This is certain, for it is the Catholic doctrine that the Blessed Virgin, like every other saint, gained heaven only as the reward of merit. Now she could not merit it by becoming the Mother of God. Her being the Mother of God is indeed a most august dignity, but there is no merit in it. It is a dignity conferred on her by the absolute decree of God, just as He resolved to confer angelic nature on angels, or human nature on men. It is no doubt a great happiness and glory for us to be men, and not brutes, but there is no merit in it; so there is honor but no merit in the Blessed Virgin's being the Mother of God. Now if she did not merit heaven by becoming the Mother of God, how did she merit it? for it is of faith that heaven is the reward of merit. I answer, by her life on earth. It was not as the Mother of God that she won heaven, but as Mary, the daughter of Joachim, the wife of Joseph, the mother of Jesus. It is impossible to read the Gospels without seeing how careful our Lord was to make us understand this. He seems to have been afraid, all along, that the splendor of that character of Mother of God would eclipse the woman and the saint. Thus once when He was preaching, a woman in the crowd, hearing his words of wisdom, and, perhaps, piercing the veil of his humanity, and thinking what a blessed thing it must be to be the mother of such a son, exclaimed: "*Blessed is the womb that bare thee, and the paps that gave thee suck,*"* but He answered immediately: "*Yea rather, blessed are they who hear the Word of God and keep it.*" No one doubts that the Blessed Virgin did hear the Word of God, and keep it. So our Lord's words are as much as to say: 'You praise my mother for being my mother; what I praise her for is her sanctity' In the same way, when they came to Him on another occasion, when there was a great throng about Him, and said: "*Behold, thy mother and thy brethren stand without, seeking thee,*" He answered: "*Who is my mother? and who are my brethren? And stretching forth his hand towards his disciples, he said: Behold my mother and my brethren. For whosoever shall do the will of my Father who is in heaven, he is my brother, and sister, and mother.*"† Ex-

* St. Luke xi., 27.   † St. Matt., xii., 48.

ternal advantages, however great, even to be related to the Son of God, are as nothing in his sight, compared to that in which all may have a part—obedience to his Father's will. Perhaps, also, this is the explanation of his language at the marriage of Cana in Galilee. When the wine failed, and his mother came to Him and asked Him to exert his Divine power to supply the want, He said: "*Woman, what hast thou to do with me? My time is not yet come.*"* He does not allow her request on the score of her maternal authority, but what He refuses on this ground He grants to her virtue and holiness, for He immediately proceeds to perform the miracle she had asked for, though, as He said, his time was not yet come. So, too, on the cross He commends the Blessed Virgin to St. John's care, not under the high title of Mother, but the lowly one of Woman. "*Woman, behold thy son.*"† Now why was this? Did not our Lord love his Mother? Was He not disposed to be obedient to her as his mother? Certainly; but it was for our sakes He spoke thus. In private, at Nazareth,

---

* St. John, ii., 4. (Archbishop Kenrick's Translation.)
† St. John xix., 26.

we are told, he was "subject to her," but on these great public occasions, when crowds were gathered around Him to hear Him preach, when He hung on the Cross, and a world was looking on, He put out of view her maternal grandeur, in compassion to us, lest there should be too great a distance between her and us, and we should lose the force of her example. He wished us to understand that Mary, high as she was, was a woman, and in the same order of grace and Providence with us. We might have said: 'Oh, the Blessed Virgin obtains what she asks for on easy terms. She has but to ask and it is done. She enters heaven as the son of a nobleman comes into his father's estate, by the mere title of blood and lineage.' But no: our Saviour says: "*To sit on my right hand is not mine to give you, but to them for whom it is prepared by my Father.*"* It is not a matter of favor and arbitrary appointment; not even my Mother gains her glory in that way. She must comply with the terms on which my Father promises heaven to men, and therefore the Church applies to her words spoken of another Mary: "*Mary*

* St. Matt. xx., 23.

hath chosen the best part; therefore it shall not be taken away from her." Oh, blessed truth! Mary is one of us. Her destiny, high as it is, is a human destiny. And she reached it in a human fashion. She built that splendid throne of hers in heaven with care and labor while she was on the earth. She laid the foundation of it in her childhood, when her feet trod the Temple aisles. She reared its pillars, when with faith, purity and obedience unequalled, she received the message of the Archangel. And her daily life at Bethlehem, Egypt, and Nazareth, her holy, loving ways with Joseph, and with Jesus, her perfect fulfilment of God's law, her interior fervent acts of prayer, covered it with gold and ivory.

Then, when the blind world was going on its way of folly; while one King Herod was deluging villages in blood, and another steeping his soul in the guilt of incest, and of the blood of the Son of God; while the multitude were doubting, and Scribes and Pharisees disputing about Christ, the lowly Jewish maiden, with no other secret but love and prayer, was preparing for herself that bright mansion in Heaven wherein she now dwells, rejoicing eternally with her Son. Oh happy news! One, at least, of our race has perfectly fulfilled her destiny. Here we can gain some idea of what God created us for. Here is the destiny that awaits man when original sin does not mar it; when co-operation with grace and unswerving perseverance secure it. The Jews were proud of Judith. They said: "*Thou art the glory of Jerusalem; thou art the joy of Israel; thou art the honor of our people.*" So we may say of Mary: 'O Mary, thou art the pride of our race. In thee the design of God in our creation has been perfectly attained. In thee the redemption of Christ has had its perfect fruit. Mankind conceives new hopes from thy success.' Christ, indeed, has entered into glory; but Christ was God. Mary is purely human, and Mary has succeeded. Why tarry we here in the bondage of Egypt? Mary has crossed the Red Sea, and has taken a timbrel in her hand and sings her thanksgiving unto God. True it is that she is fleet of foot, and we are halt and weak; but even she needed the grace of God, and the same grace is offered to us, that we may run and not faint. Listen to her song of triumph. She does not set herself above us, but claims kindred with us, and bids us hope for the same grace which she has received. *"My soul doth magnify the Lord, for he hath exalted the humble, and hath filled the hungry with good things. And his mercy is from generation to generation to them that fear him."*

Another proof that the destiny of the Blessed Virgin is substantially the same with ours, is the fact that, in Scripture the same expressions are used to describe her glory and ours. Sometimes those who are not Catholics when they hear what high words we use of the Blessed Virgin, are scandalized; but we use almost no words of the Blessed Virgin that may not, in their measure, be applied to other Saints. It is true that the Blessed Virgin has some gifts and graces in which she stands alone—as her character of Mother of God, and her Immaculate Conception—but, as I said before, these are dignities and ornaments conferred on her, and are not the source of her essential happiness in Heaven. In other respects, her glory is shared by all the Saints. Thus, Mary is called "Queen of Heaven;" but are not all the blessed called in Holy

Scripture, "*kings and priests unto God?*"* Is she said to sit at the "King's right hand?" and are not we too promised a place at his right hand, and to "*sit on thrones?*"† Is she called the "Morning Star?" and does not St. Paul, speaking of all the Saints, say, "*star differeth from star in glory?*"‡ Is she called a "Mediatrix of Prayer?" and is it not said of every just man, that his "*continual prayer availeth much?*"§ Is she called "The Spouse of God?" and does not the Almighty, addressing every faithful soul, say, "*My love, my dove, my undefiled?*"‖ Is she called the "Daughter of the Most High?" and are not we too called the "*Sons of God?*"¶ The glory of the Blessed Virgin, then, differs from that of the other Saints in degree, but not in kind. She is not separated from them, but is one of them. She goes before them. She is the most perfect of them. But she is one of them. And for this reason, the glory of the Blessed Virgin gives us the best conception of the magnificence of our destiny. When a botanist wishes to describe a flower, he selects

---

* Apoc. i., 6.   † Apoc. iii., 21.   ‡ 1 Cor. xv., 41.
§ St. James v., 16.   ‖ Can. v., 2.   ¶ 1 St. John iii., 2.

the most perfect specimen. When an anatomist draws a model of the human frame, he makes it faultless. So we, to gain the truest idea of our destiny, must lift up our eyes to the Blessed Virgin on her heavenly throne, and say: 'Oh! my soul, see for what thou art created.' Think of this my brethren, as often as you kneel before her image, or meditate on her greatness. You cannot be what she is, but you can be like her. She is a creature like you. She is a human being like you. She is a Christian like you. And her joy, her beauty, her glory, her wealth, her knowledge, her power—nay, even the mighty efficacy of her intercession—are only what, in their measure, God offers to you. "*Glory, honor and peace to* EVERY ONE *that worketh good; for there is no respect of persons with God.*" *

If these things be so, what greatness it gives to human life. Perhaps, if you had lived in the times of the Blessed Virgin Mary, you would never have noticed her; or if you had known her by sight, what would she have seemed to you but a good little Jewish girl, lowly and retiring in her manners and appear-

* Rom. ii., 10.

ance? or, later in life, a poor young woman thrust away, with her husband, from a crowded inn, or fleeing by night with an infant child? or, still later, the mother of a condemned malefactor, watching his sufferings in the crowd. Herod did not know her, and the nobles of Jerusalem were ignorant of her. She was not one of the friends of the Queen's dancing daughters. Even the rustics of the village of Bethlehem looked down on her. She carried no servants about with her, and had no palace to live in. But Faith tells us of angel visits, of union with God, of heavenly goodness, and an immortal crown. So, in like manner, how our life becomes grand and dignified when it is lighted up by faith! You know there are porcelain pictures, which in the hand are rough and unmeaning, but held up to the light reveal the most beautiful scenes and figures; so our common ordinary life, rough and unmeaning as it often seems, when enlightened by faith becomes all divine. There is a little girl who learns her lessons and obeys her parents, and tells the truth, and shuns every thing that is wicked; why, as that little girl kneels down to pray, I see a bright angel drawing near to her, and he smiles on her and says: *"Hail! Blessed art thou: the Lord is with thee."* That young man who, by a sincere conversion, has thrown off the slavery of sin, and regained once more the grace of God—what is his heart but another cave of Bethlehem, in which Christ is born, and around which angels sing: *"Glory to God in the highest; on earth, peace to men of good will."* That Christian family, where daily prayers are offered, and instruction and good example are given, and mutual fidelity is observed between the members—what is it but the Holy House of Nazareth?—the House of Jesus? Yes, good Christian, do not be cast down because you are poor, or because you suffer, or because your opportunities of doing good are limited; live the life of a Christian, and you are living Mary's life on earth. We have not, indeed, Mary's perfect sinlessness, but we have the graces of baptism, by which we may vanquish sin. We have not, as she had, the visible presence of our Lord, but we have Him invisibly in our hearts, and sacramentally in the Holy Communion. We are not "full of grace," as she was, but we have grace without limit promised to us in answer to prayer. Let us assert the privileges of our birth-right. We belong to the new creation. Angels claim kindred with us. God is our father. Heaven is our home. We are the children of the Saints—yes, of her who is the greatest of the Saints. Let us follow her footsteps, that one day we may come to our Assumption, the glory of which surpassed even the power of St. John to utter. "*Dearly beloved, we are now the sons of God, and it hath not yet appeared what we shall be. We know that when He shall appear we shall be like Him, because we shall see Him as He is.*"*

Every thing depends on our co-operating with grace. How did the Blessed Virgin arrive at such glory? By corresponding to every grace. See her at her Annunciation. The Angel comes and tells her of the grace God has prepared for her. If she had not believed, if she had not assented, what would have come of it? Why, she would have lost for all eternity the glory attached to that grace. But she did not refuse. She was ready for the grace when it was offered. She said: "*Fiat,*" "*Be it done to me*

* St. John iii., 2.

according to thy word." Oh, how much hung on that *Fiat!* an eternal glory in Heaven. So it is with us. There are moments in our lives big with the issues of our future. God's purposes concerning the soul have a certain order. He gives one grace; if we correspond to that He gives another; if we do not correspond we lose those that depended on it; sometimes, even, we lose our salvation altogether. This is the key of your destiny—fidelity to grace. You have an inspiration from God: He speaks to your soul. Oh, listen to Him, and obey Him! To one He says: 'Abandon, O, sinner, your evil life, and turn to Me with all your heart.' *"Now is the accepted time, now is the day of salvation!"* To another, who is already in his grace, He sends inspirations to a more perfect life, a life of higher prayer and more uninterrupted recollection. Another, by the sweet attractions of his grace, He draws away from home and kindred to serve Him as a Sister of Charity by the bed of suffering; or as a nun, to live with Him in stillness and contemplation; or as a priest to win souls for heaven. Oh, speak the word that Mary spoke: *"Be it done to me according to thy word."* Are you in sin? Convert without delay. Are you leading a tepid, imperfect life? Gird your loins to watchfulness and prayer. Do you feel in yourselves a vocation to a religious or sacerdotal life? Rise up and obey without delay. To-morrow may be too late. The grace may be forfeited forever. Why stand we all the day idle? Heaven is filling up. Each generation sends a new company to the heavenly host. Time is going. The great business of life remains unaccomplished. By our baptism we have been made children of God and heirs of heaven. Labor we, therefore, to enter into that rest. Mary, dear Mother, lift up thy voice for us in heaven, that we, following thy footsteps, may one day share thy glory, and with thee praise forever God the Father, Son and Holy Ghost; Amen.

SERMON XIV.

MORTAL SIN EXEMPLIFIED IN THE HISTORY OF JUDAS.

"Woe to that man by whom the Son of Man shall be betrayed."—Matt. xxvi., 24.

(A Sermon for Passion Week.)

There are some men whose crimes have made them objects of universal and eternal infamy and execration. One of these is Judas Iscariot, whose very name is a bye-word among men. Most persons seem to think that he was quite a different being from ordinary men, and was naturally a kind of evil monster, without any thing human in him. This is a mistaken opinion. There is not so great a difference between these extraordinary sinners and ordinary ones as is commonly supposed. There are a great many who have an equal degree of malice, but who have no such opportunity to show it. There are others who would become equally bad under equal temptations, but whose evil tendencies are kept under by favorable circumstances, and the absence of great inducements to wickedness. It is not probable that Judas was much worse than the common run of wilful and malicious sinners, until, by a just judgment and a dreadful calamity, he fell into the occasion of committing a crime, the greatest which ever has been or can be committed by man.

In his case, the malice that is in mortal sin is only more perfectly exhibited than in others that are less heinous. The treason of Judas is an example, first, of the evil of mortal sin as an offence against God; and, second, as the ruin of the soul.

I.

The treason of Judas is an example of the evil of mortal sin, considered as an offence against God. The gist of the offence in mortal sin lies in the turning from God to the creature. It is a renunciation of God's friendship, a desertion of his service, a discarding of his authority, for the sake of some created good which we cannot obtain without this complete desertion from God. No one ever did this, or had the chance to do it, so plainly and visibly as Judas. He was in personal and immediate attendance upon our Lord, who is God in human nature. He was the friend, the servant and the companion of the Lord in his visible and human life. He deserted and betrayed Him for a little money, for the favor of the Jewish rulers, for the sake of a more free and self-indulgent life, and to get rid of a cross he was tired of carrying. What can be a more perfect illustration of mortal sin? You have done the same, my friend, when you have denied your faith for the sake of a genteel marriage; when you have gone to a fashionable Protestant church for the sake of improving your business; when you have dropped confession for the sake of indulging with less restraint in worldly dissipation. You need not reproach Judas, for all you say against him rebounds upon yourself, and by your own mouth shall you be condemned, oh, wicked servant!

The offence of Judas was heightened by the lowness of his origin, compared with the dignity of Jesus Christ. He was a poor young man, without family, rank, or other claim on the notice of our Lord. He chose him as one of his disciples, and destined him to be one of his twelve apostles, a sharer in the glory of St. Peter and St. Paul. For such an one to betray the Master who had raised him from a station so humble to a rank so exalted was a double crime. **But it is just** what every sinner does. We have fallen by the sin of Adam into a low condition. Destitute of the nobil**ity of sanctifying** grace, devoid of all super**natural merit, without any claim** on heaven, **we have** been raised to the **rank of** children of God, as a boon of pure mercy, through the grace of our Lord Jesus Christ. And, if we then sin against God, in what respect are we better than Judas?

There was not only a great indignity in his conduct toward our Lord, but an equally great ingratitude. He owed to our Lord not only respect and obedience on account of his charracter and authority, but personal affection and gratitude on account of his goodness and kindness to him. He betrayed a friend as well as deserted a master. Oh, baseness without a parallel! But beware, lest in saying this you reproach yourself. Whenever you sin mortally you are guilty of the same ingratitude toward Jesus Christ. He has been good to you, too, and you owe Him love and gratitude. But you repay his favors with outrages and offences.

To crown all, Judas delivered up his Master to an ignominious death, and imbrued his hands in the blood not only of an innocent man, but of a friend, a benefactor, nay, more, in the blood of his Lord and Redeemer. This was a new and unheard of crime. Men had heard before of fratricide, of parricide, of regicide, but they had yet to learn of that which included all these and more, of Deicide. Strictly speaking, this crime of Deicide can never be repeated. The Son of God gave to wicked men the chance of putting Him to death, once, and only once. But every one who commits mortal sin, is guilty of a crime which partakes of the nature of the crime of Judas. Sin was the cause of the death of Jesus Christ. He died for every sinner and for every sin. Whoever commits sin, then, consents to that which caused the death of our Blessed Lord, makes common cause with his murderers, and thus becomes accessory to his death.

II.

The treason of Judas is also an example of the way in which a sinner ruins himself.

It is probable that Judas was once a faithful disciple. He had a vocation from the Lord Himself, to leave the world and follow Him. God calls to his service only those who are well disposed and fit for it, and we may, therefore, believe that Judas was at least sincere and piously inclined, before the Lord called him. He believed in our Lord's teaching, when he heard Him preach; he followed Him with constancy for a length of time; and obeyed the inward grace and outward call by which He invited him to become his disciple. As a disciple he must have been faithful, and must have shown himself worthy of a higher grace. For the Lord, who knew his heart, and always chooses fit instruments for his purposes, gave him a vocation to become a Priest, and not only that, but a Bishop and an Apostle. With this vocation He gave him all the special gifts and graces necessary to prepare him for the apostolic ministry, to make him a worthy companion of St. Peter and St. John, and to enable him to win like them, the gratitude and veneration of the world, and a glorious crown in heaven. He preached and wrought miracles like the others, and very likely was for a time not only without grievous sin, but really fervent and holy. Reason and experience teach us that he could not have changed all at once from a fervent apostle to a faithless apostate, ready to betray his Lord for money. He must have changed gradually. He relaxed by degrees in fervor, he neglected little things, and did not profit by the admonitions which the Lord gave him from time to time. Thus he went on from bad to worse, growing more indifferent and hardened every day, heaping up venial sins continually, and disposing himself for those that were more grievous. He became unkind and quarrelsome with his fellow disciples, dishonest in the use of the common purse which was intrusted to his care, harsh and repulsive toward the poor people who came to hear the preaching of his Master, and to recommend their wants to his mercy. So he lost the grace of God, fell, we know not where or how, into mortal sin, and became an alien in heart from Jesus Christ, though still in name and appearance his disciple. By degrees he began to despise his Master, to sicken of his service, to disbelieve his words. He was already a slave of Satan, having lost sanctifying grace, and, it may be, faith also. When Satan suggested to him to abandon his Master, to betray him for money, and then to go away and live as he pleased, he dallied with the temptation, deliberated, and at length consented. The devil then took complete possession of him, drove him on, and wove a chain of circumstances around him that hurried him forward to the execution of his treacherous intentions. What follows we all know. Having put the seal on his own guilt and perdition by a sacrilegious communion, he delivered over the Lord to death. His crime being now consummated, the diabolical spell that had been around him was broken, despair seized on his soul, he hanged himself and went "to his own place," bequeathing the memory of his infamous treason to the execration of all future generations.

This is the history of many a one, besides

Judas. For instance, take this from the life of St. Francis of Assisi.* "A sixth disciple, named John, and surnamed de Capella, began well, and finished ill. He was charged with distributing among his brethren the alms that had been contributed, and took on himself voluntarily the office of procuring all that was wanting for the community. But, by degrees, he became attached to temporal things, went abroad too much, and relaxed extremely in the observance of regular discipline. The holy Founder, after giving him a number of severe reprimands in vain, threatened him with a frightful malady and a miserable death, as the punishment of his indocility. In fact, this bad religious was smitten with a horrible leprosy, which he had not the patience to bear. He abandoned his companions, the poor of Jesus Christ, and giving himself up to despair, hanged himself, like Judas." This example is no doubt an unusual one, in this respect, that the penalty of this unhappy man's sinful life was more striking and visible than is commonly the case. But it is essentially like thousands of examples everywhere, and in

* F. Challipe's Life. vol. i., p. 91.

every-day life, in which the origin, progress and end of sin are really the same, though more secret and hidden. So the careless Christian begins his downward career, by a negligence which goes from bad to worse, from small things to those of greater and greater moment, until all fervor is lost, and his conscience falls into a deadly slumber. Then come grievous sins; singly at first, but afterward in quick succession. This stage of the disease lapses at last into the state of obduracy and final impenitence. Sacrilege is very commonly mixed up with it, more or less, as the religious, ecclesiastical or secular condition of the person, or his peculiar character and circumstances, may in a greater or lesser degree expose him to the occasion of profaning sacraments. He may be hurried along into an open, and perhaps, from his station and antecedents, a very scandalous apostacy from the faith, and thus become a declared traitor to his allegiance to Jesus Christ and the Church. He may fill up the measure of his wickedness in some other way; but it ends the same, in self-destruction: not by suicide, but by the gradual and sure destruction of conscience, and of moral and spiritual vitality, ending in a spiritual and eternal death which knows no resurrection forever. So he goes "to his own place," to the place he has prepared for himself, the place he has merited, the place that suits his moral condition, the place assigned to him as his eternal abode by the unerring justice of God.

This is the sinner's progress in following the footsteps of Judas. Negligence, habitual sin, contempt of divine warnings, sacrilege, obduracy, abandonment of God, despair, eternal death. At every stage it becomes harder to go back. Stop, then, where you are; or better still, if it is not too late, beware of taking the first step. If you have not yet gone very far in the downward path, and are only beginning to be negligent, take warning by the example of Judas, and correct that negligence at once, or else it may lead to the most fatal consequences. "*He that despiseth small things, shall perish by little and little.*" It is easier to preserve yourself from a great fall, by diligence and care, than it will be to remedy the hurts you will receive by falling, and to regain the height on which you are now standing. You can never tell whither any sin will lead you. You can never calculate the consequences of yielding to any temptation. Venial sins, even, may become the principle of great and fatal disorders, which will lead you to your final ruin. Threads, fine at first as spider's webs, may be so woven together, and become so strong by being multiplied, that they will entangle you in meshes which cannot be broken through without the most violent efforts. Sweep your soul, then, diligently, of these spider-webs of negligence, or you may become, like Judas, an example of one who began well, but ended miserably, and may finish that career which you commenced in the service and friendship of Jesus, by betraying both your Master and your own soul.

But even if you have already gone far in sin, it is never too late to go back, until eternal death has actually made you its prey and closed its gate behind you. The case of Judas was not hopeless until after he had placed the halter on his own neck. The Lord never ceased to remonstrate with him until that last treacherous kiss, and though after this He spoke to him no more, and Judas never saw Him again, yet He did not close the door of mercy on him even then. He closed it on himself by despairing. This was the greatest and most fatal of all his sins. Had he hoped in the mercy of Jesus Christ; had he returned to Him in sorrow and tears; had he thrown himself at the feet of his injured Master, and implored pardon, he would, no doubt, have been too late to save that Master's life, but he would have been in time to save his own soul. Even from the Cross the Saviour would have smiled upon him, and the guilt of his treason would have been effaced in that redeeming blood which his treason had made to flow. Oh! sinner, never despair! Even if you have gone to the length of an open apostasy, do not abandon hope; do not place the halter around your own neck. All is not yet lost. Retrace your steps; return to Jesus Christ; offer him the kiss, not of a traitor, but of a penitent; and you will receive from his clemency the pardon of your sins.

SERMON XV.

THE INTERIOR LIFE.

"The Kingdom of Heaven is within you."
St. Luke xvii. 21.

(From the Gospel for the 13th Sunday after Pent.)

A FEW years ago, and the people of California were a quiet, agricultural and trading people, by which they procured for themselves the three great wants of life; viz., shelter, clothing and food. They were content with as much as this, for they were unconscious that underneath their very feet, as they were working their farms and gardens, there lay that immense treasure of gold which has since been brought to this city. By chance a lucky spade turned over a clod of earth and stone, on which a yellowish tinge was noticed. It was found to be gold. The report soon found its way next door, and then about the neighborhood, and so went rapidly through the country. The cabbages and potatoes, the peas and beans, which till now had been the pride of the cottage, were pulled up without ceremony and thrown aside, in the eager search that was everywhere being made for gold. The news came over to us, and I dare say you remember well the excitement created by it here. The great tide of commerce was turned toward San Francisco, and such was the haste of our people to get there, that a crowd was daily seen pressing around the offices of the various packet and steamship lines, eager to secure an early passage.

We, my dear brethren, are living on the surface of life, with our cabbages and beans, very much as those Californians were, and all the while within our souls there is a mine of untold riches, of which we seem to be quite unconscious. We are leading a grovelling life, when we might be living an angelic one. Our condition differs as much from what it might be as the state of the caterpillar differs from that of the butterfly. They are the same creature, yet how different! The caterpillar crawls upon the ground; it feeds upon roots and leaves, and one is tempted to put his foot upon it as he passes by. The butterfly is a light airy thing on beautiful wings. It feeds upon honey which it gathers from the flower gardens, and is the admiration of every one. But before the caterpillar can become a butterfly it must build for itself a little house of silk. It must enclose itself there, and in proportion as it dies to itself, it lives again in the butterfly. My brethren, this house is your soul. There, with God, is your true life. Would that I could make you realize this. Would that I could realize it myself. Well, in order to do something toward it, I will this morning show you under what beautiful images Holy Scripture describes the beauty of a soul that is in union with God. I will name two great advantages of this union; and finally, I will tell you the conditions on which God offers it to you.

I. The beauty of a soul in union with God.

We cannot see our souls, and God has nowhere given us a description of them; but many things are said in Holy Scripture, from which we get the idea of their great beauty when united to him. The soul is called God's "Palace." This is what our Lord says in my text: "*The kingdom of God is within you.*" What is the idea that we have of a kingdom? Why, I suppose we call to mind some of the great powers of Europe, with their extensive dominions, great power and wealth. Among the cities of these kingdoms there is usually one more populous than the rest, where the streets are laid out, and the public buildings and private houses are erected with a view to magnificence; as for example: London in England; Paris in France; Vienna in Austria; St. Petersburg in Russia. The Sovereign's palace is there. This palace is grand in its proportions outside, and it is furnished within in as costly a manner as gold and silver, polished wood, rich silks and tapestry and choice paintings can make it.

Well, then, the soul must be this, and more; for it is the palace of the King of kings. Holy Angels are there in attendance upon Him. There He entertains his faithful at his table with the Bread of Angels. It is there that He deigns to hold those conversations with the soul after communion that are so precious.

St. Teresa has this same idea under another figure. She begins by saying that the beauty of the soul is incomprehensible. That the mind cannot conceive its real worth, as words cannot express it. Then she says that she conceives the soul to be like a magnificent diamond castle, with rooms above and below; but in the very centre there is a room more spacious and more sumptuous than all the others, where our Lord dwells with the soul.

The soul is God's "Temple." "*Ye are the temples of the Holy Ghost,*"* says St. Paul.

We often see engravings of those grand Cathedrals and churches which are so common abroad. There is one in almost all the old towns of England. Their tall spires or massive towers stand majestically over the country, and their whole exterior is elaborately worked in stone. On the inside they are poor and cold enough, it is true, for a false worship has been set up there, which has stripped them of their fine statuary and paintings, banners and rich hangings, which formerly decorated the sanc-

* 1 Cor. vi.

tuary and walls, and they are no longer what they once were, "the Temples of God." There is no correspondence between the size and magnificence of those churches of the olden time, and the formal service that is held in them now; and so a few square yards are penned off in the middle for the handful who will assemble. But there has been a time when those walls were too narrow to enclose the thousands who came to follow their Lord as He made the circuit of his Temple, in the procession of Corpus Christi. Those floors have been covered with kneeling multitudes who waited for his benediction in the Blessed Sacrament. Then, gold and silver, lights and flowers, massive candlesticks and rich vestments adorned the altars with something approaching to regal splendor, for it was the Temple of God. Those cathedrals and churches are now standing, after the lapse of hundreds of years, as monuments of the ancient faith that inspired their erection; but the day will come when, as our Lord said of Jerusalem, "*one stone shall not be left upon another.*" But our souls are everlasting Temples. How strong, then, as well as how beautiful, God must have made them!

The soul is a "Fountain" of never-failing water. This is what our Lord told the Samaritan woman. "*The water that I will give him shall become in him a fountain of water, springing up unto everlasting life.*"*

I think our blessed Saviour could not have said any thing which would have given us a more beautiful idea of the effect of his presence upon our souls. The deserts of the East are like the ocean in their great, boundless wastes of hot sand. Travellers tell us that for days there is no living object to be seen, even to a blade of grass. Occasionally, however, they come upon what appears like an island, where there are trees, grass and flowers. Invariably it is found that in the middle of these "oases," as they are called, there is an overflowing spring of the purest water. This is the cause of all that verdure in the midst of so barren a wilderness. How beautiful such places must be to the weary traveller, and how grateful to the eye, as he catches sight of them in the distance! How he must bless God as he sits under the cool shade of the rich foliage, or as he bathes his feverish brow and limbs in the cool waters!

* John iv., 14.

Well, our souls are so many "green islands" in the desert of this world, and our Lord is the fountain in their centre. His presence adorns the soul with all that fragrance and fulness which we find in the innocent and pure. St. Teresa had a great fondness for this passage of Scripture from her very childhood. Though at that time she did not know the value of this promise of our Lord as she did in after life, she says: "I very often asked the Divine Master to give to me this precious water."

The soul is God's "Image." *"Let us make man to our image and likeness."** So God said when he created the first human soul.

Our souls, then, are like God. God is the perfection of all beauty. As we say, God is truth, so we say, God is beauty. There are two ways in which we are like God, for He says: "Let us make man to our image *and* likeness." In one way, the devils and souls in mortal sin are like God. They have the gifts of intelligence and free will. This is the image of God which, when a creature once has, it can never lose. The likeness which a soul in the state of grace bears to God, is in the gift of

* Gen. i., 26.

habitual, or sanctifying grace. **This** can be lost, and the devils and souls in mortal sin have lost it. God has made us pupils of his, as it were. Our Master has drawn the outline of Himself upon our souls, and our work is to fill up this sketch with light and shade. A Christian is therefore an artist of the highest class; for there can be no subject so inspiring as his. What a beautiful talent it is to be able to transfer to canvas some scene from nature, of which it becomes the exact copy. There are certain combinations of water and mountain, meadow and foliage, nature and art, blended and softened by a peculiar state of the atmosphere, which act like a spell upon one. All we can say, is, how very beautiful!

But, beautiful as it is, it will vanish before the winter's frost. The canvas, too, in time will moulder away. But the image of God on our souls is more beautiful than any scene in nature, and it will preserve its beauty forever.

These are some illustrations from Holy Scripture which enable us to form an idea of what is the beauty of a soul when in union with God.

Did you ever know, my brethren, that God

had been so good to you? Have you not overlooked and undervalued your treasure? This life of yours hitherto, on the surface of things, has been both a great mistake and a great misfortune.

II. To make you realize this, let me tell you two great advantages of an interior life.

The first is, the great "peace" that it brings to us. Peace, did I say? Is it, then, possible to wear a constant smile in this valley of tears? Can these fretful souls of ours find rest even upon earth? We pray for the Holy Souls in Purgatory, "that they may rest in peace," as if we felt that there was no rest short of Heaven. Can we find it, then, even short of Purgatory? Yes, for it is a share, by anticipation, of the ineffable peace which those holy souls enjoy in the possession of God. Like them, we can be glad while we suffer. Joy and suffering are not irreconcilable! How was it with our blessed Lord? You know He is called the "Man of sorrows," in that his Passion is thought to have been before Him during the whole of his thirty-three years on earth. But all the while, his human soul was in the perpetual enjoyment of the Beatific Vision, and therefore in perfect peace. Well, of this peace, in the midst of trouble, our Lord, as the great Head, allows us, his members, to participate. Hear what He said to his Apostles: "*Peace I leave with you, my peace I give unto you.*"*

What robs a man of his peace of soul, is either an inordinate desire for something which he has not, or the fear of losing something that he has. Now, the man who lives an interior life, is in the possession of God, who is the fulness and perfection of every good. He does not fear the loss of pleasure, for his highest pleasure is to do the will of God. He says, it is not God's will that I should have pleasure now. Nor of riches, for he fears them as a snare. He does not fear poverty—he will have less to give account of at the Last Day; nor of station, for he feels that there is no nobility like being a son of God. He is living with God and his Holy Angels, as their companion; as though God and they and he were the only beings in the world. Nor of comforts, for he has learned to bear his cross, and he is learning to love it. Nor of reputation, for he seeks the favor of

* John xiv., 27.

God alone. Man's judgment of him will neither aid nor injure him before his only true Judge. The daily round of bodily weakness, sickness, disappointment, or mortification, is turned into so many occasions of gaining merit with God. It is true of him what the Scripture says, that "*all things work together for good, to those who love God.*"* He is like Midas, the fabled King of Thrace, who was said to have the power to turn every thing that he touched into gold.

St. Basil was such a man. On one occasion he was called before a magistrate, who said in great anger, " Basil, I will tear out your liver." " Well," was the meek reply, " you will do me a great favor then, for it is a great trouble to me where it is." Such a man is invulnerable.

To come nearer to our own day, I can show you such a man, in our Holy Father Pope Pius IX. What is the invariable testimony, both of Protestants and of Catholics, as to the manner of his receiving them? Every one speaks of his composure, of his cheerful conversation, and of the sweetness of his smile. Now, where is the man in Europe, who has so

* Rom. viii., 28.

much care and anxiety upon him as he has? For whom would we be so ready to make excuse, in case we were told that he was found to be reserved, or even at times out of humor, on occasion of those "receptions," which are so numerous and indiscriminate, and which we would think must be so very tiresome to him? At this moment, while Sovereigns and statesmen are threatening him with the seizure of the ancient inheritance of the Church, which is intrusted to his care, and himself with banishment, not only is he calm, but he prophesies that, from these present trials, great glory shall result to the Church. Pius the Ninth is a man who lives in close union with God. Down in the bottom of his soul there reigns a supernatural calm.

With an interior life comes also a strength to do and to suffer, which is naturally quite beyond us.

As our Lord chose his Apostles among a class of men whose natural advantages were very few, in order that his guidance and power might be shown in them, so He has adorned the early Church with a number of young female Martyrs, whose amazing fortitude under the severest torture, clearly proves that He was also the source of their strength. Let me give you an example. St. Potamiena was a Nubian slave of a Roman master. He required her consent to something which was contrary to the law of God. On her refusal, he threatened her with such torture as was exercised upon those who, like herself, had embraced the Christian faith. The magistrate before whom she was brought on the charge of being a Christian, commanded her to obey her master in all things, or she should be cast into the cauldron of boiling oil, which was seething before her. She replied: "I have but one request to make: allow my clothes to remain upon me; then, if you will, let me down by inches into this cauldron, and you will see what strength Jesus Christ, my Lord, will give me to bear its pain." This was the cruel death by which, without a murmur, she won her crown of "Virgin Martyr."

Let me give you another example of fortitude, which you can perhaps better appreciate. Some few years since, in England, there was a young lady of noble family, and of very attractive manners, who became a Religious in a convent near the town where I then resided. To please her father, she had, for several years past, attended the numerous parties that were given among her circle of acquaintance. Her presence was always thought to be a great acquisition. But all the while, her heart was in religion. She longed for the time when her father would yield, and allow her to try her vocation within a convent's walls. At last, he did; but what was his grief when he found that she had chosen one of the most austere orders in the church. She wished to become a Poor Clare. Now, you may not know that a Poor Clare never leaves the walls of her convent; she never sees any one; she walks bare-footed; she uses the painful discipline, and spends many hours of the dead of the night in prayer, while the outer world is asleep. Here, then, was a young girl who had been brought up in luxury, entering at once upon a life of the greatest severity. When I last heard of her, which was a long time after she had entered this convent, she was said to be as merry as a cricket, and the life of her convent, as she had formerly been of her parties of pleasure. Now, how shall we account for such fortitude as this? I will tell you. It was our Lord in her heart, where she had made Him a home, that gave her the courage and strength she needed to comply with his call to her, to be a spouse of his. That became easy to her, which her relatives and friends could not comprehend. There is no one who can do any thing great for God, without this interior life. I will say even more than this; neither she nor any other member of a religious community, can hope to persevere in any well-regulated convent, on any other ground than this. With this, any one, whether in religion or in the world, can trample underfoot the difficulties and trials peculiar to their state of life.

God offers us this interior life, on two conditions. In the first place, we must be in the state of grace. One must first be introduced to a man, before he can become his personal friend. A man in mortal sin is as though he did not know God. He needs to make his acquaintance. He is in a condition that is even worse than that of a stranger; he is God's enemy, and he must be first reconciled.

To drive a locomotive at the rate of forty miles an hour, one must first get it upon the track, before it will move at all.

You, then, my dear brethren, who are so unfortunate as to be in mortal sin—you can take no comfort from any thing that I have said. I have been offering peace to such as lead a Christian life; but what does Holy Scripture say of you? *"There is no peace, saith my God, for the wicked."*

Again, we must be generous with God. Ah! now that I have told you the terms, I tremble for the cause I am advocating. It seems to me that I hear you answering, as some other disciples of our blessed Lord answered him: *"This saying is hard, and who can hear it."** What is it to be generous? It is to give from a motive of love, and because it is a pleasure to give. It is to consider the object to which we are giving, rather than the amount of what we are giving. What millions of dollars are being expended on the Central Park here just beside us? We consider the money contributed, as little in comparison with the importance of the work. It is an object of pride

* John vi., 61.

with us to see this Park as ornamental as money and art can make it.

See what generous efforts are being made, by both sides, in this unhappy conflict, which has made a battle-field of our country! Not money only, but blood and life, are as freely offered as water.

Our citizens who hurried off to California at the time of the gold excitement of which I have spoken, thought nothing of the discomfort of a close state-room on board a crowded ship, for a five months' voyage. They had already sacrificed home, friends and business, and all this was on the mere chance of success.

Now, how is it with us? The burden of the sermons preached from this altar, the year round, has been merely to get *justice* done to God. We have been doing our best to get from you what is barely God's *due*. Our endeavor has been to get you to restore to God those rights of his, of which you have defrauded Him; and at best, we have had but partial success. But to-day, I ask you not for justice, but for generosity. Did I not say well then, when I expressed my fear that God would find but few who would accept his terms? On his part, He offers to come and dwell in your souls. He offers you interior peace, supernatural strength, holiness, and salvation. Now what does He ask of you in return for all this? That you will act the part of a generous friend toward Him, by giving Him a large share of your thoughts, words, and actions. He is the magnet in the centre of your hearts. He is always drawing you toward Himself. He asks that you will put no obstacle in the way of his influence upon you. If disturbing causes for the moment turn you from Him, like the needle which may be shaken so as to point to the East or the South, like it He calls upon you not to rest till you have found your rest again in Him. St. Teresa says, that a generous soul *flies* to God. She does not say that it runs, but that it flies to God. Now, what are we doing? We are content to creep and crawl toward God, like worms and caterpillars.

My dear brethren, I have told you a great truth, I have discovered to you a great treasure. It is within the reach of each one of you. Now I call upon this congregation for some companions to go with me in search of this treasure. I do not expect to arouse the mass of you, as the cry of "gold" from California aroused the people of this city. I know the sad truth, that most people love gold better than they love God. But I *do* count upon some. You would not expect that I should urge this "Interior Life" upon you, and remain myself as I am? Well then, I am going to try for it, and I call again upon you for some souls, few though they may be, who with me, will try to be generous with God. I call upon you by your Saviour's love in dying a painful and shameful death, to purchase it for you. I call upon you by his still further love in securing to you his abiding presence, in the most Holy Sacrament of the altar. Lastly, I call upon you by that act of his love which would be satisfied with nothing short of making your heart a tabernacle, as it were, where He may dwell perpetually, where He may live your life, and where you may live his life, as true children of St. Paul, who said: "*I live now no longer, but Christ liveth in me.*" I have put my question. I have made my call upon you. I leave the answer with yourselves.

SERMON XVI.

TRUE CHRISTIAN HUMILITY.

"Every one that exalteth himself shall be humbled, and he that humbleth himself shall be exalted."—St. Luke, xviii. 14.

(From the Gospel for the 10th Sunday after Pent.)

It is impossible to mistake the great moral of this parable of the Publican and the Pharisee. It is intended to teach us humility. The Pharisee, with all his pretensions to piety and morality, was rejected because he was proud. The Publican, like the generality of revenue officers in that day, was loaded with sins; but he was sorry for them, and being humble, and ready to acknowledge himself for what he was, his prayer was accepted. All piety, therefore, without humility, is false. No matter what they may say about a man's good deeds or virtues; if he is proud, he is no saint. There is no surer test of solid Christian virtue than humility. St. Philip Neri once called to see a sick Roman lady, who enjoyed a high reputation for sanctity. He found her sitting up, looking very weak, and very pious. Being desirous of putting all this perfection to the test, he lifted his dusty shoe upon the beautiful counterpane which covered the bed, and which, as it appeared to him, the good dame regarded with more than ordinary satisfaction. It turned out as he expected. He might as well have put his toe into a hornet's nest, for the pious lady was so mortified at the soiling of her counterpane that she let loose her tongue upon him in such strong Italian terms as came first to mind. "I wish you good morning, holy sister," said St. Philip. We may easily imagine what he thought of her sanctity.

Indeed, to prove the necessity of this virtue, we need go no farther than to the example contained in this day's gospel, and to the words of our blessed Lord in the text; for He tells us in plain terms: "*Every one that exalteth himself shall be humbled; and he that humbleth himself shall be exalted.*" Since, then, humility is so necessary, let us study it this morning; let us try to discover what true humility is, and to fill our hearts with the esteem of it, and the love of it.

Christian humility I understand to be this: *A lowly estimate of one's own worth in the light of Divine Truth.* This is, I am well aware, a definition of humility in the mind, rather than that of the heart; but it is not necessary to dwell upon any such distinction here, for humility of the heart is nothing else than the heart's consent to this lowly estimate of one's self, and practically speaking the two are seldom found apart.

1. Humility, I say, is a lowly estimate of one's own worth. Men are proud because they esteem themselves too highly; and this they do because they look at themselves in a false light. They look at themselves with worldly eyes, and compare themselves with what they see around them. They plume themselves upon advantages which, in the eyes of faith, are of little value. They look too low. The king sees nothing greater than himself, and looks down upon the nobles; the nobles look down upon the untitled gentry. We have neither

king nor nobles in our country, but we have a class of gentry who live upon fortunes made by their fathers, and were reared in good society. These look down upon those who have made their own fortunes by some honest trade. The tradesman looks down upon the farmer, the farmer upon the hired laborer, and the laborer who has a shanty, with a cow and pigs, finds some one still poorer to look down upon; and this last, perhaps, is proudest of all, for he is descended from some patriot of the Revolution, or, it may be, from Brian Boroihme. If, on the contrary, they would look at the sacred law of God, if they would study the pure and holy lessons of the Gospel, if they would raise their eyes upward to the high and heavenly destiny for which they were created—if by this new light they would compare themselves as they are with what they might be, and ought to be, the trifling advantages of this world would disappear, their pride would wither away, and give place to humility, the earliest, if not the sweetest flower of the Christian year.

But how is it with those who are *spiritually* proud? Do not they estimate themselves by

12*

the light of faith? **No.** Their pride would soon die out if they did. Faith, directing their eyes upward, would discover to them in God, in Jesus, and in the Saints, what true holiness is, and their poor store of sanctity would show like thumb-marks in a prayer-book, or spots upon the sun. In the darkness of a cloudy night, when only the nearest objects that lie about your feet are visible, your thoughts are bound up in that little circle as if all the universe were near you and beneath you, and you walking on its summit; but when the clouds are driven away, and the moon and the vast world of stars appear, the heaven seems like a measureless dome, and you, a little insect creeping upon the floor, look up in breathless wonder. So the pathway of a conceited devotee is lighted only by a few straggling rays of religious truth, and he sees himself shining as a luminous point in that narrow circle which is visible to his eyes; but let faith open the sky above him, and give him one long, calm, thoughtful look at the world above, and he stands rebuked and humbled. Oh! how little our virtue appears when, instead of comparing ourselves with the worldly crowd around us, we look up to see how the saints have lived, and what they have done!

During the Moorish wars in Spain, while the Spaniards were besieging a city of the Moors, a brave Castilian knight advanced before his comrades, at great peril of his life, and for a memorial of his valor, wrote upon one of the city gates: "Hitherto came Vasco Fernandez." His companions were scandalized at his pride, and anxious to teach him a lesson. The next day, therefore, another hero of superior prowess forced his way still farther, and wrote in large letters upon another gate: "Hitherto Vasco Fernandez did not come." This, my dear brethren, is a lesson for the Christian soldier also, and well worth learning. Instead of comparing ourselves with the feeble and imperfect, and feeding our pride thereby, let us humble ourselves before the achievements of the Saints.

2. If humility is a lowly estimate of one's-self, it is none the less truthful on that account. We must look upon ourselves as we really are, "in the light of Divine Truth," for this is included in my definition. One may think meanly of himself upon false grounds. One

may be ashamed of himself for things which in reality are praiseworthy. There is no virtue in this. Genuine humility needs to borrow no aid from falsehood. She is a grace bestowed by the God of truth. Now, there is something very unhealthy and degrading in this spurious sort of humility, which is founded upon self-calumny and pious exaggeration, for it leads to self-degradation. And this is the reason why I abhor the Protestant doctrine of "total depravity." It teaches men to say that they are, from their birth and by nature, so thoroughly corrupt, that there is absolutely nothing good in them. That there is, in reality, no such thing as natural virtue. That filial piety, honesty, fidelity, love of truth, chastity and temperance, have no merit in the unregenerate man, but, on the contrary, are sinful and displeasing to God. And their doctrine of justification leaves the Saint as bad as the sinner; for although his life is acceptable with God, it is not because he is in reality any better, or that his actions are more meritorious. On the contrary, his righteousness is all "filthy rags," and there is positively nothing good in him. He is justified and saved by faith alone.

If you say to them, "Ah, well, I understand you; this faith of which you speak is at least something meritorious, because it is enlivened and made holy by charity, or the love of God. It is this which makes faith so efficacious." No; they will not admit your explanation; there is popery in it; it is only an entering wedge to make way for the doctrine of good works. They refuse to accept any principle by which the good man may be supposed to be really any better than his neighbors. He is regenerated by the mantle of Christ's righteousness, which does not take away, but only covers up his "filthy rags." And his lesson of humility is, to insist upon it that there is nothing good in him. Now, I never saw any one, either man or woman, so bad that I thought there was no good in him; and I am always sorry to hear my Protestant friends speak so ill of themselves, for I don't believe them—I have seen too much real merit among them.

In truth, all this is false humility. It is but a form of words, and nobody in his heart believes it, or can believe it. Virtue is not vice. There is such a thing as real virtue and real merit in man. God has given to all a conscience, which is nothing else than His own voice applauding or rebuking. There is such a thing as natural virtue, which deserves a reward in the natural order of God's providence; and there is such a thing as Christian virtue, which is begotten by supernatural grace, and deserves the supernatural reward of the Saints.

No wonder that, in the world, humility is too often looked upon as a counterfeit and degrading virtue, which takes away all manliness, hope, courage, and generous ambition, from the soul. Oh, if it were so, I would suffer my tongue to be torn out of my mouth, before I would preach it at this altar. If ever there was a time when we needed manly virtue in the Church, it is now. If ever there was a time when Christianity seemed to have melted into effeminacy and pusillanimity, it is now. The race of Martyrs, of Confessors of the faith, of Christian athletes, of true Sages and sacred Scholars, of men of action who knew how to open their eyes, and men of prayer who knew how to shut them, of Catholic Matrons and Virgins whose hunger after holiness was not satisfied by crosses and medals, scapulars and holy water—this ancient race of Christians has well nigh dwindled away. We of the present day seem to be playing with religion. We are not in earnest. We are ashamed of what ought to be our glory; we are proud of that which constitutes our shame. We have no blushes for our sins; while we are too bashful to be devout, and too timid to practise virtue. We acknowledge that we are wicked; although we do not hold it to be precisely our own fault, but a fault of our nature, and we have no ambition to be better. We confess our sins by throwing all the blame upon the God who made us, and this we call humility. Oh! this is false humility. God made us well enough; our sins are all our own. If we look at ourselves as we really are, in the light of divine truth, we shall find matter enough to make us humble.

3. True Christian humility, so far from degrading, ennobles the heart in which it dwells. It leads directly to hope; and hopefulness is, in all great hearts, the essential element of their courage, energy, enterprise, and success. Now Pride, with her two brazen-faced daughters

Self-conceit and Self-confidence, stands directly in the way of Christian hope and courage. In spiritual matters, so long as one depends upon himself, he is sure of failure; for without the grace of God one cannot advance a single step. "*Without Me*," said our Lord to His disciples, "*you can do nothing.*"* With repeated failure comes despair, or at least, despondency; and then all hope, courage, and generous enterprise take flight. But how different is the experience of the humble heart! It begins with self-distrust; it acknowledges its own feebleness. "*For I know,*" says the Apostle Paul, "*that there is no good dwelling in me; that is to say, in my flesh. As for the will to do good, that I find present, but the power to do it I do not find.*"† Not daring, therefore, to trust in himself, the humble Christian learns to lean upon God, and to confide fully in his grace; and then he becomes strong and full of courage, and can say with St. Paul, "*I can do all things through him who strengthens me.*"‡ Thus, in the Christian warfare, humility is the first and last lesson of all noble, generous, and heroic souls; for their

* St. John xv., 5.   † Rom. vii. 18.   ‡ Phil. iv., 13.

great hearts are sustained by great hopes, and their hope is nourished by humility.

Humility, and that hopefulness and courage which grow out of humility, are also the most efficacious means of converting the shamefaced, downcast sinner. Take, for example, the habitual drunkard. The pledge will not help him long; and why? Because he is degraded in his own eyes, and has no confidence in his own resolutions. What he wants most is courage, and the pledge cannot give him that. The pledge teaches him to rely on himself, and on himself he cannot rely. "I'm willing," says he, "but I'm weak. If you are going to give me the pledge, put it on me strong, so that I won't break it." See how the poor fellow is anxious to find some support to lean upon, outside of his own weak will, and is almost ready to believe that the priest can give him that stability which he so much needs. Now, what is to be done? The only way is to put confidence and courage into his heart; and this is done by pointing him upward to God, the only source of grace and strength, and "*who is able to do all things*

* Ephes. iii., 20.

*more abundantly **than** we can ask."** Do not take the heart out of him by words of contempt and scalding abuse, but speak to him kindly and encouragingly. "I know, my dear friend, that you are weak; but God is strong, and his grace is able to make you strong. He has had worse cases than you in hand before now, and made glorious Saints of them too. Never despair; you were created for better things. Make one more trial now, and with the help of God you'll shake off this miserable habit forever." That's the way to reform a confirmed drunkard who has grace enough, at least, to be ashamed of himself. Do not strike a man that is already down. Do not make him more self-degraded than he is, but out of his humiliation endeavor to fill him with hope in God. Talk to him cheerfully. Give him a clean shirt and a clean collar. Get him to wash himself and shave himself, and brush his hair. He will now begin to feel like a man; and the next step is to feel like a Christian. Take him then to the Church, and to confession; and when upon his knees, with a contrite heart, he has confessed and renounced his sins, let him there pledge himself against that drink which has poisoned him, body and soul; and the grace of God will carry him through. In this way, courage and strength are born of humility. It is a virtue that does not degrade, but ennobles the heart where it lodges.

I have said enough, I think—all, at least, my dear brethren, that can well be said within the compass of a morning's sermon, to illustrate the true nature of Christian humility. I need not enlarge upon the advantages or the necessity of it. Humility is one of those sweet virtues which carries its own recommendation with it, which needs only to be seen in order to be prized. Enough has already been said to justify that maxim of the ascetic writers, that humility is the foundation of all the virtues. Any mason will tell you, that before you can build a substantial Church you must dig away the loose dirt below, and hollow out a foundation for the walls. This is the first step of all, and until this is done, neither walls, nor tower, nor roof, nor any part of the building can be safely undertaken. It is the same in that spiritual temple which has to be erected in every soul that is saved. Before we build up we must first go down. Humility must first begin the work; must dig up and throw aside the sand and rubbish of pride, and self-conceit, and vain confidence, which have gathered like a loose soil upon our hearts. Then, and not till then, are we ready, with faith, and hope, and charity, and the other virtues, to rear the strong walls, and towers, and arches, with all the parts and ornaments which make the Temple of God complete within our souls. In fine, religion is of little use to one who will not learn to be humble; and therefore an English poet, varying the figure which I have employed, says very well:

> "Ye who would build the churches of the Lord,
> See that ye make the western portals low!
> Let no one enter who disdains to bow!"

If any thing were needed to confirm this view of the necessity of humility, we have the words of our Lord himself: "*Unless you be converted and become as little children, ye shall not enter into the kingdom of Heaven.*"*

Are we then, my brethren, anxiously desirous of saving our souls? Would we be some-

---

* St. Matt. xviii., 3.

thing in the kingdom of God? Would we become strong in faith, great in hope, abounding in charity? Then let us cast pride away! Let us learn to be humble! Let us become willing imitators of Jesus Christ, who has said: "*Learn of me, for I am meek and humble of heart, and you shall find rest to your souls.*"* And let us believe his word, that there is no other way of salvation; for He it is who tells us in this day's Gospel, that "*every one that exalteth himself shall be humbled; and he that humbleth himself shall be exalted.*"

* St. Matt. xi., 29.

SERMON XVII.

WHAT THE DESIRE TO LOVE GOD CAN DO.

"Thou shalt love the Lord thy God with thy whole heart, and with thy whole soul, and with all thy strength, and with all thy mind."—St. Luke x., 27.

(From the Gospel for the 12th Sunday after Pent.)

There are two ways in which one may set about fulfilling this commandment of the Lord.

The first way is, to do what is barely necessary in order that we may be said to fulfil it at all. The second way is, to fulfil it in its perfection, according to the most generous meaning of the words. When may one be said to fulfil it in the first way? When he has a firm determination to keep clear, at all times, of every mortal sin. It is plain, that in this case he can be said to fulfil the commandment, because, after all, he prefers God to every thing else. When he determines to avoid every mortal sin, no matter what the temptation to commit it may be, he does give his whole mind and heart to God in some sense —at least, really and substantially, though it may be imperfectly. If he does not go that far, he does not in any sense fulfil this commandment. He loves the sinful thing more than he loves God. He is ready to give up God, rather than his will and pleasure. His whole heart and soul loves sin—is turned away from God. He cannot entertain any hope of eternal life: that is clear from the words of the Saviour in to-day's Gospel. The Lawyer asked Him, "*What shall I do to possess eternal life?*" The Saviour said, "*What is written in the law? how readest thou?*" He answered: "*Thou shalt love the Lord God with thy whole heart, and with thy whole soul, and with all thy strength, and with all thy mind.*" And the Saviour replied: "*Thou hast answered right, this do and thou shalt live.*" You see what the condition is. We must fulfil this commandment, or there is no eternal life for us. Let us not deceive ourselves. If we cannot honestly and sincerely say: 'I am determined to keep clear of every mortal sin,' our religion is vain. Don't build on the idea that we shall be saved because of the Catholic faith we profess. "*Think not,*" says Jesus, "*to say, We have Abraham for our Father. Do penance; the axe is laid to the root of the tree; every tree that bringeth not forth good fruit shall be hewn down and cast into the fire.*"* But is it enough just barely to fulfil the commandment in this way? No, it is not. One who does not go farther, runs a very great risk of being lost. The fact is, to maintain one's self in an habitual horror of mortal sin requires a great deal of fervor and recollection. In order to do so, one must also aim at avoiding every deliberate sin, small or great; one must really be in earnest to please God, or, in other words, one must strive to fulfil the commandment of the text with a good degree of perfection. That is plain enough to the dullest comprehension. A man may get over an ordinary difficulty well enough, but when a great one comes in his way, he requires all his strength and resolution to overcome it. So the ordi-

* St. Luke iii., 8, 9.

nary temptations may be avoided, but there come times which try the soul, great temptations, or unusual difficulties, and great fervor is necessary to overcome them. They come just when least expected, when one is off his guard. Unless one maintains himself, then, in this state of fervor, so as to be prepared for these occasions, he must fall. A ship that is strong enough for fair weather, goes down in a strong gale of wind. A drowsy sentinel may serve as well as another for awhile, but when suddenly beset by an enemy, is slain before he can get ready to defend himself; so the Christian, who goes on the principle of keeping clear of mortal sin, but makes light of lesser sins, will be sure to come to a grievous fall at last. "*He that despiseth small things,*" the Scripture says, "*shall fall by little and little.*"* The man who goes on the principle of gratifying his passions as much as he can short of mortal sin, will never stop there. He will overleap his boundary, as surely as the sun goes down at the close of day, as surely as the water that eats out the sand from the foundations of a house will

* Ecclus. xix, 1.

finally bring it to ruin. Such a person is not only in danger of ruin in the world to come, but loses the peace and consolation which the servants of God ought to have in this world. There is too much selfishness about him. He is trying to join together two things as contrary as God and the world—an impossibility, as God Himself says: "*No man can serve two masters, for either he will love the one and hate the other, or he will hold to the one and despise the other. Ye cannot serve God and mammon.*"*

Now, the Lord intended to remove these evils, to show us a sure and safe way to everlasting life, and to fill our souls habitually with a heavenly peace and consolation, by enjoining on us to fulfil this commandment with perfection, and, as the words sound—"*with all our hearts, and with all our souls, and with all our mind, and with all our strength.*" I think this is enough to prove conclusively the necessity of such fulfilment; now let us see how it is to be done.

But, at the very outset, a great repugnance and distaste will arise, I doubt not, in the

* Matt. vi., 24.

minds of many, at hearing these strong words of the text. It will seem to be asking too much—more than they can dream of fulfilling. In their idea, it would seem an impossibility, even if they had the best will in the world. "What," says the father of a family, "give my whole soul and mind to God? To take care of my children, to put bread in their mouths and clothes on their backs, takes up, and must take up the principal part of my time and attention. I must attend to my business, and use all my skill and prudence and activity to make all things meet. I cannot do as the old hermits of the desert did, pass my time in constant prayer and meditation." "What," says the mother, "give all my strength and all my mind to God! How can I do it? I must expend all my strength going up and down stairs, in the kitchen, in the dining-room, in my own room sewing and mending, to keep every thing decent for the children. I must teach them, and look out for them. One thing or another takes up my time and attention the whole day, so that, when night comes round, I am glad enough to get to bed and to sleep as quick as I can." "What," says the young woman, just growing out of her girlhood, "give my whole heart to God, when this dear old world is so pleasant, and I have such fine times in it?" Alas! not the young woman only, but the young man, and the old man and the old woman, too, are apt enough to speak in this way. Dissipation and pleasure keep such a hold upon them, that they seem to be more giddy and foolish as they grow older. And another cry comes up from all quarters: "How can I give my whole heart and soul to God, when the troubles and sorrows of the world, its cares and anxieties and disappointments fill me with bitterness and rage, and excite every evil passion? In this miserable world there is no such thing as tranquillity or peace, and how, without these, can the whole heart be given to God?"

Now, dear brethren, whoever you may be who speak or who think in this way, put down that feeling a little while; listen with patience while I propose to you a means of fulfilling Christ's commandment which will smooth away these difficulties, and enable you to do so in a manner most pleasant and agreeable to you. I do not pretend that this means takes away from you all necessity of exertion—all effort and care to do right. No, the words of Christ must hold true: "*Strive to enter into the straight gate,*" He says. "*Fight the good fight,*" says St. Paul. The prize of our high calling is too valuable to be had without being in earnest about it. But I can venture to say, that by the method I propose, it is by no means so difficult a thing to fulfil Christ's commandment as you may suppose; that, with a little patience and perseverance, it will become an easy and agreeable thing to do so. What is this method? It is—*to excite and keep in your souls an ardent desire to love God.*

This desire will do every thing, if it is strong and lively. Now, the desire to love God is a thing natural to the soul. How so? Why, thus. We naturally desire what is good—what will conduce to our interest, our pleasure or profit. We express this by the very word "desirable." As soon as we become acquainted with the value of any thing to us, we desire it, and our desire for it is in proportion to our appreciation of it. So a good name is more desired among noble-minded men than the possession of riches—a substantial wealth, more than the pleasure of the senses. Now, what is more desirable than God? To possess Him, is to possess all that is good, all that is beautiful, all that is honorable, all that makes happiness. As soon as we know, even imperfectly, what God is, a strong desire to possess Him must arise in the soul. It may be transitory, quickly fade away and lost sight of, through the things of the world which occupy the attention, but, whenever we reflect on it, that desire must—it is impossible that it should not—rise up in the soul. This transitory desire, which passes away like a vapor, is of little or no value; it does not last long enough to produce any practical impression. It is what is called a *velleity*, or ineffectual wish, if it is not nourished and made permanent, so as to influence one's life.

But since this desire to love God is natural to one who knows what He is, it must be, therefore, an excellent and easy means to acquire a high degree of that love. It is like the oar in the hands of the rower. It is like the wing by which a bird mounts high in the air. Why, as soon as this desire acquires force enough to control the will (and any strong desire is sure to do so), we cannot separate the desire to love God from the love of God itself. God does not measure our love to Him by our feelings, for we may seem to ourselves to have little, while our will shows that we love Him dearly. The trouble then with us, and I may say our only trouble is, that we do not enough desire to love Him; that we do not keep that desire bright and lively in our souls. Surely we have abundant reason for it! Besides the loveliness of God attracting us, our eternal destiny depends upon it—heaven and hell. Only let us turn over in our minds the vast importance of loving God, and we must be compelled to cry out with intense desire: "Oh, that I did love God with all my heart, with all my soul, with all my mind and strength!" I say, then, excite this desire; think, and think every day, on these simple things: Who am I? Who is God? What has God made me for? What is the world and all in it, compared to the love of God? Or, as the Gospel reads, "*What shall it profit me to gain the whole world, if I suffer the loss of my soul?*" Perhaps this fire of desire is almost out in your soul; but there is still fire there—there is one coal at least burning yet. Blow it into a flame! Keep on blowing, and that fire will be sure to spread, until the whole heap is in a blaze. You see, all that is required of you is to think, to reflect. Put your mind upon it with earnestness; and the desire of God must speedily gain the mastery of your soul. When it does so, it will regulate all its motions, and make every thing that was before so unnatural and difficult seem wonderfully easy.

Let us see how it would fare then with sin. Only keep that ardent desire to love God burn- in your soul, and you will find it a very hard thing to commit any deliberate sin. It is a maxim in physical science that two bodies cannot occupy the same space at the same time. One must displace the other. So, I say, two strong desires, that are opposed to each other, cannot stay together in one heart. Either one or the other must give way and yield posses- sion. So our Lord said long ago under cover of this comparison: "*When a strong man armed keepeth his court, those things which he possesseth are in peace. But if a stronger than he cometh upon him and overcome him; he* *will take away all his armor wherein he trusted, and distribute his spoils."** The strong desire for God's love will take away from the desire for sin all its armor, all its strength, and leave it powerless to hurt us. It had a peaceable possession of the soul before, because nothing seriously disputed its right to govern, but now the desire to love God has made it hateful and loathsome. The strong man has become weak as an infant. When we fix our eyes on sin, perhaps its allurements, and the force of old habits, may make it so attractive, that it would gain the mastery once more. Certainly it would make a desperate struggle for the mastery. But let us look up to God! Let us consider how necessary, how desirable in every view is his love, until we become resolved that at least we will long for it, and continue longing for it, as long as life is long; saying with the royal Psalmist: *"As the hart panteth after the fountains of water, so panteth my soul after thee, O God."** Then will all those allurements and attractions of sin vanish. We shall only wonder how such miserable things could have blinded us so long.

* St. Luke xi., 21, 22.   * Ps. xli. 1.

We all know how strong and engrossing the passion of earthly love is. The lover is taken with some real or fancied perfection of his mistress, either a beautiful face, a noble figure, or, it may be, with what is far more to be prized, some noble qualities of the mind or disposition. His whole mind is taken up with her night and day, and his only study is, how he may recommend his suit. If encouraged with the prospect of success, transports of joy fill his soul; if met by neglect and indifference, he is plunged into the deepest melancholy. If parents or relatives put obstacles in the way, heaven and earth are moved to get them out of the way. This is the burden of so many novels and romances that are read with eagerness by people of every condition and every class of society. If the desire of earthly beauty, of body or soul, so imperfect, so unsatisfying, so short-lived, can thus engross the soul of man, why should not the desire of God's love, who is perfect beauty, perfect wisdom, perfect goodness, and our promised portion for ever and ever, be able to do far more? It will remove all obstacles out of the way. We shall say, as did St. Agnes to her admirer and tempter: "Depart from me thou food for death, for I am betrothed to Him whom the angels serve, whose beauty sun and moon admire." Every creature that breathes is food for death. Sin is the food of eternal death. The idea that mortal sin brings eternal death, eternal separations from this infinite beauty and goodness, must make us regard it with the same horror that fills the soul at the sight of a ferocious tiger or deadly serpent. It will make the occasions of sin hateful, and cause the soul to exclaim: "Away from me, ye frightful temptations! I know you: Ye bear the serpent's tongue and the tiger's claw. Ye carry with you the risk of God's anger and my eternal ruin." Who that loves God, or desires to love Him, could venture into any place, into the society of any person, where the danger of mortal sin is lurking, since he knows that mortal sin is banishment from God?

This sacred desire would also consume every kind of deliberate sin, whether great or small. This is the language of a heart that longs after divine love. "Oh! how can I admit this, it is sinful; it will cool away the fervor of my soul, it will prevent me from making that near approach to God's love which I so much covet." Cursing and swearing, lying, slandering, pilfering, and every form of dishonesty, all immodesty in deed, word or thought, anger and foolish pride—how would these all disappear before such a fervent desire! And all this would be accomplished without any violence to the soul, quietly, but powerfully and effectually, and even with delight and satisfaction. For is it not a joy to follow where our heart's desires lead? But this holy desire leads toward God, and away from sin.

Again, this ardent desire to love God more and more will make it easy and pleasant to us to perform all our duties. We cannot work without a motive, without proposing something to ourselves which appears good in our eyes. If the work to be done is arduous or difficult, the motive or inducement must be a strong one. Such a strong motive will render what is difficult easy. How easy it is for men to take the longest journeys, endure the greatest labors, when their souls are fired with the desire of providing for their beloved ones at home, or with a noble ambition to serve their country, or even for the miserable pursuit of gain. Only hold out the prospect of success, and any amount of labor seems light to them. Cannot the motive of God's love do as much? Is it not as great? Can it not fill the soul as much as any other? For an answer to these questions, look at what the Saints, holy men and women, have done. Urged and animated by this all-absorbing love, they have not counted life even as dear to them, but given it up freely and gladly under the most frightful torments. Look at the labors and sufferings of others, for example, of a St. Francis Xavier, enough in his case, one would suppose, to kill twenty ordinary men, all endured with the most heroic cheerfulness and joy. No, depend upon it, the labors and duties of ordinary life will seem trifling in the eyes of the Christian who longs for the love of Jesus Christ. His soul burns for opportunities. 'What shall I do?' he says. 'Why do I stand here idle? Lord, send me something to do.' The cares, duties, and responsibilities of every-day life are the first things to be done; sent by the Lord to be done for his sake. Therefore the soul, instead of finding in them a source of complaint, finds an outlet for that activity which she **desires** to exercise for God. Suppose one would only say to himself, 'I want to do something to please God and increase in his love. **Now,** I have not to search for it; it is here before my face. To take care of my family, endure fatigue and exertion for them, to discharge with fidelity this office or employment committed to me, by which I earn my bread. I will set right to work to do it. It is little indeed that is required of me, but that little, and nothing else, **is what God** requires of me now. Thanks be to Him who has made my way plain before my face.' In this way do things naturally distasteful and irksome become agreeable, when the love of God is spread over them.

This desire for God's love will also moderate all excessive desire for the pleasures of the world. I do not speak now so much of sinful **pleasures, as of** allowing the heart to go too much after such as **are allowed. Such** liberty leads to **sin by a short road.** Our life is too important **to be trifled away.** God requires of us not to set our hearts on the pleasures or pomp of **this world,** because then it is sure to forget, what is of so much more importance, Himself. Now, as soon as the soul in earnest perceives that indulgence is producing this effect, that she is losing the relish for the love of God and spiritual things, she is startled, and cannot but feel afflicted. 'What,' she says, 'shall I barter away so immense a good for such trifles? The very pain this reflection causes weans her away from pleasure. She judges, and judges rightly, that a small enjoyment neglected for so high a motive, will bring a higher and better happiness. We all know this in every-day affairs. Most men prefer to neglect the pleasure of the moment when they see that they gain a greater one for themselves in the future. How provident, how temperate they are in early life to lay up an abundance for old age! What old age can compare with eternity? How strong then the motive of the soul to moderate all her earthly desires, that she may have time and opportunity to look out for that eternity. The ardent lover of God looks at every thing in such a light. Pleasure becomes irksome to him very soon, because he has something so much more important on his mind, that he cannot, and will

not rest easy, unless it be attended to. He is no longer a little child, and cannot amuse himself with running after butterflies the whole day. Besides, a greater pleasure has engrossed and filled up his soul, and leaves no room for trifles. It is the happiness of uniting himself to God. There is no drawback to this. After a day spent in trying, with all his heart, to please his God, he feels no regret for it at night, when he lies down on his pillow. He is not left uneasy, restless, and dissatisfied, as when pleasure, ease, and self-indulgence were his aim, but is full of tranquillity, full of hope, and full of the desire that his whole life may be thus spent in the same, or greater efforts, to please God. The pleasures of the world soon grow to be worthless in the eyes of such a man. With St. Paul he says: "*I account all things as dung, so that I may win Christ.*"*
It is not hard to part with what we esteem so little. The joy of the heart amply compensates for all sacrifices, so that instead of a long face, a melancholy and soured heart, such a one enjoys deep gladness and satisfaction of mind, which grows deeper and more complete,

* Phil. iii. 8.

in proportion as he is weaned away from the pleasures of the world.

Finally, all those things which are naturally disagreeable, such as misfortunes, pains, sickness, trials of all kinds, become easy and even agreeable through such a strong desire. The Martyrs smiled in the midst of their torments. Did they not feel them? Most certainly they had the same flesh and blood as ourselves. But their souls had a sight of Jesus, surrounded by his Angels, and this distracted their attention from all their torments. So St. Stephen, when he saw this sight, became radiant with joy, and his face shone like the face of an Angel. Sufferings, tribulations and trials are things that force the soul to look steadfastly upon Jesus, and the sight of Him takes from them all their bitterness. So we read that an old hermit of the desert complained when his yearly sickness failed to come upon him, that the Lord had neglected to visit him. The soul that earnestly desires God's love needs only to be told that pain of body or mind, borne patiently, as coming from God's hand, is the surest means of obtaining its desire. Pain is accepted then with alacrity, and with pleasure.

To be sure, the first pangs may be exceedingly hard to bear; the soul may require a little time to recollect herself, and gather force to overcome the repugnance of nature. But a little reflection puts every thing in its proper place. 'Shall I,' she says, 'reject the very things I have longed for, the opportunities of making rapid progress in the love of God?' If this does not still the tumult of nature, prayers are resorted to, and in the end comes victory and triumph, a wonderful vigor and refreshment of the soul.

This is not merely for Martyrs and canonized Saints; it is a thing that belongs to every-day life—the grand remedy for all the ills we are subject to: "*Take up my yoke,*" says the Saviour, "*for my yoke is easy and my burden light, and ye shall find rest for your souls.*"* It seems strange that the cross of Christ should give rest, but it is so; and the tribulations which come from his hand, as St. James says, work patience, and patience hath a perfect work; therefore it is to be counted joy to receive them, and not sorrow. And such will be the sentiment of the lover of God. So in the Sermon on the

* St. Matt. xi., 29.

Mount, the burden is always: "*Rejoice and be exceeding glad.*" For what? Poverty, afflictions, persecutions, false testimony, and so on—they are worthy of joy, because they bring what the soul so much desires.

See then what great things the desire to love God will do for you! May the poor thoughts which I have strung together, excite in your minds this fruitful and wonder-working desire. Regard the love of God as the pearl of great price. Consider over and over again the value of it. Persevere in efforts to appreciate it. Say to yourselves—I will not forget. I will continually repeat: 'Oh, God, make me to know thee, and to love thee more and more! Oh, how I wish to love my God better than I do!' Excite this desire in the morning when you arise—during the day, when you are tempted—when you are discouraged—when you have any thing to suffer—in the midst of pleasure, and whenever the Holy Ghost inspires it. At night, take some time to reflect upon the love of God, to sigh and beg for it. Persevere, and it will not be long before your heart will be inflamed with it—your whole life will be filled with it. Your only uneasiness will be because that burning desire cannot be fully satisfied in this world. This is to hunger and thirst after justice. What a blessed hunger and thirst it is, and what a blessed promise accompanies it! "*Blessed are ye who hunger and thirst after justice, for you shall be filled.*"* Filled with justice! What does that mean? Filled so that we shall not want any more. Not filled with money—which will leave us poor and naked at the last hour. Not filled with sensual pleasures, which please the heart in time and burn it in eternity; but filled with justice, that is, filled with God—filled with a deep inward peace and joy during our mortal life—a foretaste of heaven; and filled with glory and happiness unspeakable in heaven itself forever. Amen.

* St. Matt. v., 6.

SERMON XVIII.

THE WORTH OF THE SOUL.

"There shall be joy before the angels of God over one sinner doing penance."—St. Luke xv., 10.

(From the Gospel for the 3d Sunday after Pent.)

THIS is what theologians call an *accidental* joy. The essential joy of Heaven consists in the perfect knowledge and love of God, and is unchangeable and eternal; but the accidental joy of Heaven springs from the knowledge of those events in time which display the goodness and greatness of God. The first of these events was the creation itself, when the hand of God spread the carpet of the earth and stretched the curtains of the heavens. Then "*the morning stars praised Him together, and all the sons of God made a joyful melody.*"*

* Job xxxviii., 7.

After this the great historic events of the world have been successively the burden of the angelic songs—the unfolding of the plan of Redemption, the birth of Christ, the triumphs of the Church. But lo! of a sudden these lofty strains are stopped. There is silence for a moment, and then the golden harps take up a new and tenderer theme. What is it that has happened? What is the event that can interrupt the great harmonies of Heaven, and furnish the Angels with a new song? In some corner of the earth, in some secret chamber, in some confessional, on some sick bed, in some dark prison, a sinner is doing penance. He prays, whose mouth had been full of cursings. He weeps, who had made a mock at sin. The slave of Satan and of Hell turns back to God and Heaven—and that is the reason of this unusual joy. It is not that a recovered sinner is really of more account than one who has never fallen, but his recovery from danger is the occasion of expressing that esteem and love for the souls of men which always fills the heart of God and the Angels. Therefore, as that contrite cry reaches heaven the Angels are silent, for they know that there is no music in the ear of God like that. And then, when God has ratified the absolving words of the priest, and restored the contrite sinner to His favor, they cast themselves before the throne, and break forth into loud swelling strains of ecstasy and triumph, while He Himself smiles his sympathy and joy. Oh, my brethren, what a revelation this is! A revelation of the value of the soul. There are great rejoicings on earth when a battle is won, or upon the occasion of the visit of some great statesman or warrior, or when some great commercial enterprise is successful, but these things do not cause joy in Heaven. The conversion of one soul—it may be a child, or a young man, or an old woman—the conversion of one soul, that it is that makes a gala day in Heaven. Now God sees every thing just as it is, and if there are such rejoicings in Heaven when a soul is won, what must be the value of a soul! Let us confess the truth, we have not thought enough of the value of a soul. We have thought too much of the world, of its pleasures, of its profits, of its honors, but too little of our own souls. We have not thought of them as God thinks of them. Let us then strive to exalt our ideas, by considering some of the reasons why we should put a high value on our souls.

In the first place, we should value a human soul, because it is in itself superior to any thing else in the world. The whole world, indeed, with every thing in it, is good, for God made it. But He proceeded in a very different manner in the creation of the material world from what He did when He made the soul. He made the world, the trees, the rivers, the lights of heaven, the living creatures on the earth, by the mere word of his power. "*God said, Be light made. And light was made.*"* And God said, "*Let the earth bring forth the green herb, and the fruit tree yielding fruit after its kind. And it was so.*"† But when He made the soul, the Scriptures tell us, "*He breathed into the face of man and he became a living soul.*"‡ By this action we are to understand that God communicated to man a nature kindred to his own divinity. The Holy Ghost, the Third Person of the Blessed Trinity, is the uncreated Spirit of God, eternally breathing forth and proceeding from the Father and the

* Gen. i., 3.   † Gen. i., 12.   ‡ Gen. i., 26.

Son; and God when He breathed into the face of man, signified that He imparted to man a creative spirit kindred to his own eternal spirit. The Holy Scriptures indeed, expressly tell us that such was the case; "*Let us make man to our Image and our Likeness.*"* This likeness consisted in the possession of understanding and free will, the power of knowledge and love—the two great attributes of God Himself. You are then, my brethren, endowed with a soul which raises you immeasurably above God's material creation. You have a soul made after God's image. This is the source of your power. The two things go together in Holy Scripture. "*Let us make man to our Image and Likeness: and let him have dominion over the fishes of the sea, and the fowls of the air, and the beasts, and the whole earth, and every creeping creature that moveth upon the earth.*"† In the state of original innocence, no doubt, this dominion was more perfect, but even now it exists in a great degree. "*Every kind of beast, and of birds, and of serpents, and of the rest, is tamed, and hath been tamed by mankind.*"‡ See how a little boy can drive

* Gen. i., 26–27.   † Gen. ii., 7.   ‡ St. James iii., 7.

a horse. See how a dog obeys his Master's eye and voice. See how even lions and tigers become submissive to their keepers. And the elements, often wilder than ferocious beasts, are obedient to you. The fire warms you and cooks for you, and carries you when you want to travel for business or pleasure. The wind fans the sails of your vessels, and the waters make a path for them under your feet. Even the lightning leaps and exults to do your bidding and to be the messenger of your will. Thus every thing falls down before you and does you homage, and proclaims you lord and master. What is the reason that every thing thus honors you? It is on account of the soul that is in you—the power of reason and will—the godlike nature with which you are endowed.

Yes, and your soul is the source of your beauty, too. In what consists the beauty of a man? Is it a mere regularity of form and feature? Do you judge of a man as you do of a horse or a dog? No; the most exquisitely chiseled features do not interest you, until you see intelligence light up the eye, and charity rradiate the countenance—then you are captivated. A man may be a perfect model of grace in his movements without exciting you, but when he becomes warm with inspirations of wisdom and virtue, when his words flow, his eye sparkles, his breast heaves, his whole frame becomes alive with the emotions of his soul, then it is you are carried away, you are ready almost to fall down and worship. What is the reason that Christian art has so far surpassed heathen art? the Madonna so far more beautiful than the Venus de Medicis? It is because the heathens portrayed the beauty of dead matter; the Christians portrayed the beauty of the soul. And if the soul is so beautiful in the little rays that escape from the body, what must it be in itself? God has divided his universe into several orders, and we find the lowest in a superior order higher than the highest in the inferior order. The soul, then, is more beautiful than any thing material. "*She is more beautiful than the sun, and above all the order of the stars: being compared with the light she is found before it.*"* Oh, my brethren, do not admire men for their form, or their dress, or their grace, but admire them

* Wisdom vii., 29.

for the soul that is in them, for that is the true source of their beauty.

It is also the secret of their destiny. God did not give you this great gift to be idle. He gave it for a worthy end. He gave understanding that you might know Him, and free will that you might love Him; and this is the true destiny of man. You were not made to toil here for a few days, and then to perish. You were made to know God, to be the friend of God, the companion of God, to think of God, to converse with God, to be united to God here, and then to enjoy God hereafter forever. Once more then, I say, do not admire a man for his wealth, or his appearance, or his learning. Do not ask whether he is poor or rich, ignorant or learned, from what nation he springs, whether he lives in a cabin or palace. Let it be enough that he is a man, possessed of understanding and free will, spiritual and immortal, with a soul and an eternal destiny. That is enough. Bow down before him with respect. Yes, respect yourselves—not for your birth, or your station, or your wealth, but for your manhood. "*Let not the wise man glory in his wisdom, and let not the strong man glo-*

ry in his strength, and let not the rich man glory in his riches. But let him that glorieth glory in this, that HE UNDERSTANDETH AND KNOWETH ME."* Yes, my brethren, this is your true dignity, the soul that is in you—the soul, that makes you capable of knowing and loving God.

And yet, there is another reason why you should value your souls, besides their intrinsic excellence—I mean, the great things that have been done for them. Do you ask me what has been done for your souls? I ask you to look above you, and around you, and under you. Oh, how fair the earth is! See these rivers and hills! Look on the green grass! Behold the blue vault of heaven! Well, this is the palace God has prepared for you above; nay, not for your abode—your dwelling-place is beyond the skies, where "*the light of the moon is as the light of the sun, and the light of the sun seven fold, as the light of seven days,*"— but for the place of your sojourn. This earth was made for you; and, as your destiny is eternal, therefore the earth must have been made to subserve your eternal destiny. Why does

* Jer. ix., 23, 24.

the sun rise in the morning, and go down at night? It is for you—for your soul. Why do summer and winter, seed-time and harvest, return so regularly? It is for you, and your salvation. The earth is for the elect. When the elect shall be completed, the earth, having done its work, will be destroyed. This is the end to which, in God's design, all things are tending. God does not look at the world, or its history, as we do. We say: "Here such a great battle was fought;" "there such a celebrated man was born;" "in this epoch such an empire took its rise, such a dynasty came to an end." But God says: "Here it was a little child died after baptism, and went straight to heaven;" "there it was I recovered that gifted soul, which had wandered away into error and sin, but which afterward became so great in sanctity;" "in such an age it was that I lost that great nation which fell away from the faith, and in such another, by the preaching of my missionary, I won whole peoples from heathenism." I know we shrink from this in half unbelief. When it is brought home to us that this little earth is the centre of God's counsels, and our souls of the universe, we are amazed and offended. But so it is. "*All things work together unto good to them that love God.*"* All things; not blindly, but by the overruling Providence of Him who made them for this end.

Do you ask me what has been done for your souls? I answer, the Church has been established for them. Look at the Church, and see how many are her officers and members—Bishops, Priests, Levites, Teachers, Students. All are yours—all are for you. For you the Pope sits on his throne; for you Bishops rule their Sees; for you the Priest goes up to the altar; for you the Teacher takes his chair, and the Student grows pale in the search for science. That the Apostolic commission might come down to you, St. Peter and St. Linus and Cletus ordained Bishops in the churches. That the true doctrine of Christ might come down to you uncorrupted, the Fathers of the Church gathered in council, at Nice, and Ephesus, and Chalcedon, and Trent. That you might hear of the glad tidings of Christ, St. Paul and St. Patrick labored and died. For you, for each one of

* Rom. viii., 28.

you, as if there were no other, the great machinery of grace, if I may express myself so coarsely, goes on.

Do you ask what has been done for your souls? Angels and Archangels, and Thrones and Dominions, and Principalities and Powers —all the hosts of Heaven—have labored for them. *"Are they not all ministering spirits, sent to minister for those who shall receive the inheritance of salvation?"** For you the whole Court of Heaven is interested, and one bright particular Angel is commissioned to be your guardian. For you St. Gabriel flew on his message of joy to the Blessed Virgin Mary, and St. Michael, the standard-bearer, waits at the gate of death.

Do you ask what has been done for your souls? From all eternity God has thought of them, the means of salvation been determined on, the chain of graces arranged. And the Son of God has worked for them. Galilee, and Judea, and Calvary were the scenes of his labors on earth, and on his mediatorial throne in heaven He carries on still his unceasing labors in our behalf. And the

* Heb. i., 14.

Holy Ghost has worked. He spake by the Prophets, and on the day of Pentecost He came to take up his abode in the Church, never to be overcome by error, or grieved away by sin, to vivify the Sacraments, and to enlighten the hearts of the faithful by the preaching of the Gospel and his own holy inspirations.

Why, who are you, my brethren? The woman at Endor, when she had pierced the disguise of Saul, and knew that she was talking with a king, was afraid, and *"said with a loud voice: 'Why hast thou deceived me, for thou art Saul?'"** So, I ask you, who are you? I look upon your faces, and I see nothing to make me afraid; but faith tears away the disguise, and I see each one of you radiant with light, a true prince, and an heir of heaven. I look above, and see Heaven open and the Angels of God ascending and descending on errands of which you are the object. I look higher yet, and I see God the Father watching you with anxiety, and the Son offering his blood for you, and the Holy Ghost pleading with you, and the Saints and Angels, some with

———
* 1 Kings xxviii., 12.

folded hands supplicating for you, and others pointing with outstretched hand to the glorious throne reserved in Heaven for you.

Have you, my brethren, so regarded yourselves? Have you valued that soul of yours? Have you kept it as your most sacred treasure? Is it now safe and secure? Oh, how carefully do men keep a treasure they value highly! Kings spend many thousand dollars yearly just to take care of a few jewels. The crown jewels of England are kept, as you know, in the Tower. It is a heavy fortress, guarded by soldiers who are always on watch. At each door and avenue there is an armed sentinel. The jewels themselves are kept in glass cases, and visitors are not allowed to touch them. And all this pains and outlay to take care of a few stones that have come down to the Queen by descent, or been taken from her enemies! And that precious soul of yours, before which all the wealth of the world is but worthless dross— with what care have you kept that? Alas! every door has been left open. No guard has been at your eyes to keep out evil looks. No guard at your ears to keep out the whispers of temptation. No guard at your lips to stop the way to the profane or filthy word. Nay, not only have you kept up no guard, but you have carried your soul where soul-thieves congregate. The Holy Scripture says: "*A net is spread in vain before the eyes of a bird.*"* Yes, the birds and beasts are cunning enough to avoid an open snare; but you go rashly into dangers that are apparent to all but you. Sinners lie in wait for you. They say, in the language of Scripture: "*Come, let us lie in wait for blood; let us hide snares for the innocent without cause. Let us swallow him up alive like hell, and whole as one that goeth down into the pit*"—and you trust yourself in their power. Oh, fly from them! Consider the treasure you carry. "*What shall it profit a man to gain the whole world and lose his own soul?*" Will you sin against your own soul? you that are made after God's likeness; you that are princely and of noble rank, will you defile that image, and degrade yourselves to a level with the brutes that perish?

But there are others whose offence is of another kind. They let their salvation go by sheer neglect. If a man plants a seed, he must

* Prov. i., 17.

water it, or it will not grow. So the soul needs the dew of God's grace; and prayer and the Sacraments are the channels of God's grace. Yet how men neglect the Sacraments! Even at Easter, when we are obliged to receive them, some absent themselves. It has been a matter of the keenest pain to us to miss some members of this congregation during the late Paschal season. You say, you have nothing on your conscience, and it is not necessary to go to confession. But is it not necessary to go to Communion? Will you venture to deprive yourselves of that food of which, unless ye eat, the Saviour has said: "*Ye have no life in you?*" Oh! you have a sad story to tell. You have fallen into mortal sin, and you are afraid to come. But do you think we have none of the charity of the Angels? Only convert truly, for it is a true conversion that gives the Angels joy, and we can give you the promise that Thomas à Kempis puts into the mouth of Him whose place we fill: "How often soever a man truly repents and comes to me for grace and pardon, as I live, saith the Lord, who desireth not the death of a sinner, but rather that he should be converted and live, I will not remember his sins any more, but all shall be pardoned him."

And to you, my brethren, who, during the Easter season just past, have recovered the grace of God, I have a word of advice to give in conclusion. Keep your souls with all diligence. Keep your souls; that is your chief, your only care. Keep them by fleeing from the occasions of sin. Keep them by overcoming habitual sins. Nourish them by prayer and the sacraments. How great a disgrace, that all the irrational world should do the will of God, and you, the rulers of the world, should not do it! *"The kite in the air hath known her time; the turtle, and the swallow, and the stork have observed the time of their coming; but my people have not known the judgment of the Lord."** How great an evil it is in a State when an unworthy Ruler is at its head. The people mourn and languish, and at last rebel. So, when a man neglects the end for which he was made, the whole creation cries out against him. The stones under his feet cry out. The air he breathes, the food he eats, protest against the abuse he makes of them.

* Jer. viii., 7.

Balaam's ass rebuked the madness of the Prophet; so when you live in sin, the very beasts reproach you. Your horse, your cow, your dog, your pigs cry out: "If we had souls we would not be as you. Now we serve God blindly, and of necessity; but if we had souls, it would be our pride and happiness to give Him our willing service." All things praise the Lord;—"showers and dew;" "fire and heat;" "mountains and hills;" "seas and rivers;" "beasts and cattle." O, sons of men, make not a discord in the universal harmony! Receive not your souls in vain! Serve God; "praise Him and exalt Him forever."

SERMON XIX.

MERIT THE MEASURE OF REWARD.

"Behold, I come quickly; and my reward is with Me, to render to every man according to his work."—Apoc. xxii., 12.

Society is made up of numerous classes of persons, of very varied position and attainments. How marked is the line, for instance, which divides the man who lives in the Fifth Avenue, anywhere below Fortieth street, from the occupant of a shanty on the outskirts of the city! Again, what point of contact is there between the man of science or literature, whose life is spent in intellectual pursuits, and the vacant lounger that hangs around our steamboat landings and wharves? These men move in separate spheres, and have scarcely any thing in common. They are like two different races of men. The difference is perhaps less marked in this country than elsewhere, inasmuch as royalty and nobility and hereditary titles do not exist here. But even in this country there is a clear line of division between distinct classes of persons. Shall this always be so? Shall these accidental and artificial barriers survive death? How will it be in heaven?

No, my dear brethren, these particular lines of division, of rich and poor, learned and unlearned, shall cease with this world; but others will be set up in their place. There is an aristocracy, there is a hierarchy, in Heaven. St. Paul, after saying, "*There is one glory of the sun, and another glory of the moon, and another glory of the stars, for star differeth from star in glory,*" adds, "*so also is the resurrection of the dead.*"* St. Teresa calls this difference "a prodigious inequality." We must not imagine, however, that these various ranks of glory in Heaven are founded upon such accidents as birth or good fortune. They are founded upon that proportion of merit which we shall have gained, each one by his

* 1 Cor. xv., 41, 42.

good deeds in this life. The amount of grace and personal holiness that we possess when we appear in judgment before the Lord, this, and not wealth, or position, or gifts of any kind, will be the standard by which we take a high or low place there. It is about this principle of "personal merit" before God, and in view of Heaven, that I am going to speak to you this morning. In order to do this, I shall speak of the certainty of merit, of the sources of merit, and the conditions of merit.

I. The Certainty of Merit.

What is meant by merit? It is that supernatural reward, which God has promised by way of justice, to a good work done in the state of grace. God has made a contract with us, as it were, in virtue of which He has given us the privilege of claiming eternal happiness from Him on certain conditions. Let me show you how this is the teaching of Holy Scripture. "*Rejoice and be glad, for great is your reward in heaven.*"* Our Lord, you see, uses the word reward which I have used. "*Every one*

* St. Matt. v., 12.

shall receive his own reward according to his labor.* St. Paul here adds another idea to that of reward, namely, that it shall be given according to one's labor, or good works. This is what our Lord says in the words of my text: *"Behold I come quickly, and my reward is with me, to render to every man according to his work."* *"For the rest there is laid up for me a crown of justice, which the Lord the just Judge will give me in that day; and not to me only, but to them also who love his coming."*† In this passage St. Paul tells us another truth about the principle of final rewards. He says they shall be given by way of justice. The time for mercy will then have passed, and we shall be weighed in the balance of justice, and our reward shall be in strict proportion to the weight of merit we have cast into the scale. *"Therefore, my beloved brethren* (he writes to the Corinthians), *be ye firm and immovable, always abounding in the work of the Lord; knowing that your labor is not in vain in the Lord."*‡ Then, there is that passage of which I have already spoken, where St. Paul illustrates the diversity of rewards. *"For*

---

* 1 Cor. iii., 8.   † 2 Tim. iv., 8.   ‡ 1 Cor. xv., 58.

there is one glory of the sun, another glory of the moon, and another glory of the stars; for one star differeth from another star in glory. So also shall it be in the resurrection from the dead."

Thus from Holy Scripture we get these several facts with regard to the rewards of the next life, namely, first, that it is a reward, and not merely a favor from God. Next, that it is a reward for good works. Thirdly, that this reward is given by way of justice. And lastly, that these rewards differ as widely from one another as do the several lights of the sun, moon, and stars. But of what use is Holy Scripture to us without Her interpretation, whose office it is to interpret, as it has been to preserve it? I will quote you two, out of many, decrees which the Holy Church made on this matter at the Council of Trent. "If any one shall say that the just ought not for their good works done in God, to expect and hope for an eternal recompense from God, through his mercy and the merits of Jesus Christ, if so be that they persevere to the end in well doing, and in keeping the Divine commandments, let him be anathema." Again, "If any one shall say that the good works of a justified man are in such sense the gifts of God, that they are not also the merits of the justified man himself, let him be anathema."

It is then certain, both from Holy Scripture and from the decisions of Holy Church, that **we can merit the** possession of heaven as a right, by our good works. But you will say, if this be true, does it not tend to cherish in us a spirit of self-sufficiency, and of independence of God? No, it does not; **and for the reasons I am now going to give you,** in speaking on the second point, namely:

II. THE SOURCES OF MERIT.

There **are two sources** of merit, neither of which **are in ourselves, but** both of them are in God. **One is** the goodness of God; the other, the merits of Christ.

1. My brethren, God is not bound to his creatures except so far as He has been pleased to bind Himself. He could have lived on as well without **any creation** at all. And even now that he has created our race, his promise is the only **measure** of our rights and privileges. These promises were forfeited by our first pa-

rents, and God might never have renewed them to us, their posterity. But " *God so loved the world as to give his only begotten Son, that whoever believeth in Him may not perish, but may have life everlasting.*"* " *Behold what charity the Father hath bestowed upon us,*" says St. John in his Epistle, " *that we should be called, and that we should be the sons of God.*"† It is because we are sons of God, "and joint heirs with Christ," that God has honored us so much, and made it possible for us to merit by our good works. In order however, to keep us humble and to make us mindful that in all things we are indebted to his goodness, God has reserved to Himself two graces which we cannot merit, and without which we cannot be saved. These are the gifts of sanctifying grace and of final perseverance. A man is not likely to take airs upon himself and be insolent to you, when he is lying on the broad of his back in the road, and cannot stir hand or foot to help himself. No, he is most likely to address you in terms of supplication and entreaty. Well, this is our condition when God, of his pure

---

* John iii., 16.   † St. John iii., 1.

love, bestows upon us the gift of sanctifying grace. Then, again, though we should have this gift to-day, we may lose it to-morrow, and but for God's continued graces we would infallibly lose it. Can you imagine a dependence which is more pure than ours is upon God? An infant is not more dependent upon its mother for the preservation of its physical life, than we are upon God for our spiritual life. "Give us this day our daily bread," is our every morning prayer. We are like little birds in a nest before that they are able to fly. All we can do is to make a piteous cry, and hold up our mouths to be filled. Where, then, is there room for presumption in such teaching as this? Now, let me go on to my second source of merit, which is the merit of Christ.

2. We are in a double sense indebted to our Blessed Lord. He is not only our Creator, our Preserver, and our Benefactor, but He is also our Redeemer. It is by his bitter Passion and Death, and in union with these, that what we do in his name has a value and a price in the sight of the Eternal Father. It is that precious Blood of his which is poured into our soul in holy Baptism; it is that precious Blood of his

which we drink in Holy Communion, that constitutes the pure and holy source of every good and meritorious act of ours. He has Himself explained how this is, in the parable of the vine. "*I am the vine, ye the branches. He that abideth in Me, and I in him, he beareth much fruit.*"* Let us now try to get at our Lord's meaning. It is quite common nowadays to see a grapery in a gentleman's country garden. The entire roof of those ornamental glass-houses is covered with luxuriant vines; and they in turn are loaded with rich green leaves, and with beautiful bunches of grapes. The sap has made its course through the length of the vine, and into the various branches. Here it has forced out a green leaf, and there a bunch of fruit. These it continues to feed, by a continuous flow, until the leaf has gained its size and color, and the fruit its delicacy of flavor. Both leaf and fruit owe their existence, their beauty, and whatever is excellent in them, to this sap, which is the source of all; but will you say that they do not have these things in themselves? Will you say that the grapes are not really fine flavored, but only

* John xv., 5.

called so because they belong to an excellent vine? No, certainly not. You say the grapes are fine, because they really are fine, because they answer in point of taste to what you understand by that term. They have in themselves a something which is not accidental to them, but which is an essential quality in grapes of that kind, namely, that delicate flavor which has established their worth.

Now, apply this to ourselves. We are united to our Lord through the Sacraments, as branches to a vine. His grace is that precious Sap which has been let in upon our souls, through those seven main channels. They cleanse and purify our souls. They sanctify them, and make them beautiful and pleasing to God. The acts of the soul, so long as it is united to God by this divine gift of grace, are at the same time the acts of grace. They are good and meritorious, inasmuch as they are done by the co-operation of grace with our intelligence and free will. By rewarding such acts as these, God rewards the works of his own hands. This is what St. Augustine says: "When God crowns our merits, He does no more than crown his own gifts."

Let me illustrate this in another way. St. Paul says, in his second Epistle to the Corinthians, "*I have espoused you to one husband, that I may present you as a chaste virgin to Christ.*"* Here he calls the soul the wife, and Christ its husband. By this we are to understand, that the grace of Christ in the soul enables it first to conceive good desires, and then to bring forth good works, which are, as it were, the children of the soul. Thus a dignity and worth are communicated to them, which are, in a true sense, divine. Suppose, for instance, a Prince of royal blood were to marry a peasant girl. Her children would unquestionably have royal blood in their veins, however obscure may have been the parentage of their mother. They would be entitled to the right of succession, and could claim the throne of their father. Well, in like manner our good works, having God as their Author, are able to claim from Him a supernatural reward.

III. The Conditions of Merit.

There is one condition of being able to do a good supernatural work, which always comes

---

* 2 Cor. xi., 2.

first, and that is, that the person shall be in the state of grace when he does it. God can find no pleasure in us so long as our will and affections are turned away from Him, and this is the case when we are in mortal sin.

Again, our merit will be in proportion to the excellence of the work in itself considered. One apple is better than another, though both have grown upon the same branch. To attend the bedside of some poor sick person, is a more excellent work than merely to bestow an alms upon him. To be contrite for one's sins, is more excellent than to do penitential works in expiation of them. To forgive the injury of one's enemy, is more excellent than to pardon the unkindness of an acquaintance. The poorest effort at self-control, is better than the best advice given to another. I remember a story which shows what even one excellent work will do for a soul. It is in "The Lives of the Fathers of the Desert." A monk, who was serving God with much prayer and self-denial, was tempted with the desire to see a man whose merit in the sight of God should be the very counterpart of his own. God gratified his weakness. He was directed to go to a certain inn in a neighboring village where he would see such a man. On reaching it, there stood before the door a poor fiddler playing for pennies. The monk understood, by an interior light, that this was the man. Much surprised, and rather mortified too, he nevertheless addressed the fiddler, and asked him what sort of a life he had led, and what he was then doing for God? He answered, that he had, for many years, gained a poor but honest livelihood in the same humble employment. That as to his having done any thing very good, he did not know about that, although there was one thing that he always remembered with a great deal of satisfaction. "With some danger to myself, I once rescued a poor girl from those who would have ruined her." The good monk was made to understand, that for preventing that outrage, God had raised this poor fiddler to a great purity of soul.

A good work, again, is more excellent in proportion as it is more difficult. What a consolation this ought to be to us! How hard we think it sometimes to get on in life, with its multiplied vexations and discouragements!

We say, "What a strange world!" "What a weary world!" In the language of Holy Scripture we say, "*In the morning, who will grant me evening? and at evening, who will grant me morning?*"* as though things were turning out very different from what we had a right to expect. Ah! God has been good to us in the planning out of our lives, better than we should be, if we had all the planning to ourselves. I have shown you that future rewards are to be determined by merit; now our merits are measured by our trials. By your own admission then, this world, in being full of trials, most completely answers the end for which God created it. If we could but get into the habit of looking at things from this point of view, the face of life would be lit up with a perpetual sunshine. Yes, the harder our state of life is to bear, the more difficulties we find in following our Lord, the more laborious the work, so much the brighter are our prospects for the life to come, if we prove faithful to the end. How well the mother of the Maccabees, that noble woman, knew this! Holy Scripture says:

* Deut. xxviii., 57.

"*She was to be admired above measure, and worthy to be remembered by good* men, *who beheld her seven* sons slain in the space of one day, *and bore* it with a good courage for the hope she had in God."* As the youngest, her last and dearest, was about to be put to death, she encouraged him to be resolute; and he went to a martyr's reward under the influence of a consoling thought, which he thus beautifully expressed: "*My brethren having now undergone* a short pain, are under the covenant of eternal life."

Again, our merit is in proportion to the purity of the intention with which we do the work. The intention we make, either actual or habitual, is the chalice, as it were, in which we make our offerings to God. It is even more than this; for the excellence of the intention is imparted to the work itself, and becomes the measure of its merit. I once saw some wooden goblets in the window of an apothecary shop. Being curious to know what they were for, I was told by the clerk that they were made of quassia, a peculiar kind of wood which imparted to pure

---

* 2 Maccabees vii., 20.

water, when drank from these goblets, a most healthy tonic. Now, so it is with a pure intention. If the work that we do for God is only pure and good in itself, the intention will communicate to it its own peculiar excellence, and the work will receive the reward of that excellence, which has become its own.

Suppose, for instance, you hear Mass from a mere motive of duty, as being a Catholic. It is a supernatural work, and it will secure a supernatural reward. But to that intention you have added another the next time you hear Mass; namely, the intention of doing penance for your sins. Well, the same act is now doubly meritorious. The third time you hear Mass from a pure desire to make reparation to our Lord for all the injuries He has received in the Blessed Sacrament, and your intention is more excellent still, and, if united with the other two, will merit a three-fold reward.

Again, great merit is gained by small things done for God. This is surely very encouraging for us who have not the abilities, or the opportunities, of doing great things. Of course I mean great things as the world views them. A check put upon a wrong thought; the arrest of an improper word; the silence to which we have forced ourselves, when we feel within us the swelling of anger; the call we make upon a sick neighbor in passing; the alms we bestow, however small; the effort to be patient under sickness or pain; the kind word of advice to the erring; each such act as these, will be a passport at the gate of Heaven.

And now, dear brethren, I repeat once more what I said when I began. There is an aristocracy, there is a hierarchy, in Heaven. As there are nine choirs of Angels, and, so St. John tells us, except "the one hundred and forty four thousand" who had consecrated their virgin bodies as first-fruits to God, none could sing the "*new song*" or "*follow the Lamb whithersoever he goeth,*" so shall it be forever.

I will say more; and this is what I wish especially to impress upon your minds. You must already have gathered it from what I have said. It is this. That aristocracy, that hierarchy, is in process of formation at this moment. It is not determined by an arbitrary choice in heaven, but on the principle of personal merit, here on earth. How is it with a large body of students at one of our colleges or universities? They are class-mates, or even room-mates, for years, but look at them after the lapse of twenty years, and what are their respective positions? One is a merchant, in a small way, in a country town of a new state; while the other is representing his country as Minister at a first-class foreign court. One is a village physician, while the other is the nation's choice to fill the Presidential Chair. So shall it be with families. Some will scarcely be saved, while others will fill up the ranks of the seraphs, which were broken at the time of Lucifer's rebellion. Where, I ask, shall our place be in this hierarchy? Our Lord says: "*The last shall be first, and the first last.*" Where shall we be? Grace and a good will are the only materials wanting in the formation of a Saint Aloysius, a Saint Stanislas, or a Saint Elizabeth of Hungary; and these are in the reach of every one. What shall I say in conclusion, dear brethren, to spur you on to do good works? I will ask you to look back upon the past. Does it not lie in your memory in all the blackness and barrenness of a western prairie, over which the desolating fire of the savage has passed? Where can you find the trace of any real care of your souls? Where your good works? Where your merit? At least let us resolve now, while our hearts are warm, that we will improve the present, remembering that "*what things a man shall sow, those also shall he reap;*" and that "*he that soweth in the Spirit, shall reap life everlasting.*"*

* Gal. vi., 8.

SERMON XX.

SELF-DENIAL.

"We came into the land to which thou sentest us, which in very deed floweth with milk and honey, as may be known by these fruits."—Num. xiii., 28.

(A Sermon for the first Sunday in Lent.)

WHEN the ancient people of Israel, after traversing the desert of Arabia, drew nigh to the promised land of Canaan, Moses, their prophet and leader, sent out one of every tribe to view the country, that they might be able to bring back an accurate account of it—of its productiveness, the number and strength of its population, and its means of defence. These spies, upon their return, were all agreed in regard to the wonderful fertility of the country, but in other respects their account was very discordant. One of their number, Caleb the son of

Jephone, was full of enthusiasm, and said to the people: "*Let us go up and possess the land, for we shall be able to take it!*" But the others that had been with him spoke ill of the country, representing it as unhealthy, and impossible to be conquered. "*The land which we have viewed devoureth its inhabitants; the people that we beheld are of a tall stature. There we saw monsters of the sons of Enac, of the giant kind, in comparison of whom we seemed like locusts.*" Why did these last give such a different account from the first? It was because they were cowardly, and afraid of the inhabitants of Canaan, and this blinded them to the fertility of its soil, its fine fruits and great beauty. Their fears caused them to exaggerate difficulties, and to overlook blessings which were within their reach.

This party of pusillanimous Israelites represent a portion of the Christian world in our day, who, taking counsel of their fears, and consulting their ease, speak of the practice of self-denial, and the virtue of penance, as something to be dreaded, unnecessary, and even criminal. "*It is a land which devoureth its inhabitants!*" They imagine insurmountable obstacles in the way. "*We saw there monsters of the sons of Enac, of the giant kind.*" If their souls were of a more robust make, if their hearts were a little larger, their error would be dispelled, and they would see that a life of Christian mortification, instead of devouring them, would introduce them to the enjoyment of spiritual advantages and pleasures such as they never yet conceived of. They would find it a land "*which in very deed floweth with milk and honey, as may be known by these fruits.*"

Their error concerning the virtue of Self-denial is owing in some measure to a misconception of its true meaning. To establish its true meaning, let us ask ourselves first of all, what is a true Christian life? The little catechism tells us that man was created to know God, to love Him and to serve Him in this world, and be forever happy with Him in the next. A true Christian life, then, consists in knowing, loving and serving God. If we give any other direction to our thoughts, or affections, or actions, we live falsely. Self-denial, as a Christian virtue, consists in renouncing all misdirection of the powers of the soul, or in setting aside all things which stand in the way of our realizing the great end for which we were created. Complete self-denial places the soul in true and complete relations with God.

Man has become in a great measure the servant and slave of the appetites and passions of his inferior nature, and by every act of self-denial he recovers his lost superiority, and renders himself again their master. Whenever, therefore, we find our passions and appetites are leading us astray, we should resist them, and practise self-denial and mortification. If a man, for instance, finds that his sensual appetites lead him to gluttony and drunkenness, he should fast and practise sobriety. If pride and vanity are entering his heart, he should exercise himself in humility. When he finds that the love of riches is making him miserly, he should be liberal to the poor. Anger must be overcome by meekness, incontinence by chastity, and sloth by vigilance and action. Briefly, the office of self-denial is to deny to the instincts of our lower nature what is contrary to right reason, and to God's holy law.

Should there, however, arise conflicting claims between our higher and lower nature, then the renunciation of one good for another of a higher order must be practised; according to the words of Christ: "*If thine eye scandalize thee, pluck it out, and cast it from thee.*"* For what, after all, are created things, or the **members of a man's** body, or even his life, compared with the eternal salvation of his soul? **Men** do not hesitate to sacrifice the less to save the greater; to cut away the masts of a ship in a storm to save the vessel; to amputate a limb to save the whole body. It is on this principle that our Lord **declares that,** "*It is better for thee that one* **of thy members** *should perish, than* **that thy** *whole body should go* **into hell.**" Again our Lord says, on the same point, "*If any man come to me, and hate not his father, and mother, and wife, and children, and brethren, and sister, yea, and his own life also, he cannot be my disciple.*"† The meaning **of our Lord is not that there is** in these human ties any thing contrary to God's law, for his commandment to us is, "Honor thy father and thy mother;" "Love thy neighbor as thyself." The meaning of the text is; if your father, or your mother, or your wife or children, or your

---

* St. Matt. xviii., 9.   † St. Luke xiv., 26.

brother or sister, or even your own life, should stand in the way of your duty to God, then they must be subordinated, or even sacrificed, to your obedience and duty to Him. Our duty to God is supreme; and when the question arises of obeying Him or clinging to something else we possess or prize, He is content with nothing less than an unconditional surrender. So, then, self-denial is practised not to deny one's self of any thing that is a real good, but in regulating what is disorderly, in repressing what is excessive, in renouncing what is evil, that we may come in possession of our sovereign good. It aims at restraining the excesses of our animal instincts, and holding them in subjection to reason, and not at their destruction. For, in themselves considered, there is nothing even in our animal instincts which is irreconcilable with the perfection of the soul.

The same may be said of all human relationships; if they are not made to stand in the way of our salvation, and the keeping of the Divine Law, they render our natural life the more complete, and the obligation for their renunciation ceases. Did not Christ look upon mankind with human eyes, and make all our human feelings his own? As a son He obeyed his mother until his death; and even while suffering on the cross, such was his filial love and solicitude for her welfare, that He gave her in charge to his beloved disciple. As a friend, He wept at the death of Lazarus. In fine, all human sympathies, sorrows, and woes, found a home in his bosom. No, there is nothing in all created things, nor in human nature, even in its lowest appetites and passions, which may not be brought into harmony with reason, be reconciled with what holds the first place in the rank of our duties, and be made to contribute and adorn the perfection of the soul.

For it is not the purpose of Christianity to supersede man's nature; it supposes his nature. Christianity would be of no account independent of human nature. Christianity finds us men, and leaves us men; gentle, not cowardly; child-like, not childish; amiable, not effeminate; zealous, not fanatical; earnest, not narrow-minded; pious, not weak; humble, not abject; full of faith, and yet rational; obedient, not slavish; mortified, not mutilated; for Christ died to save man, and not to transmute man into something else. Christianity demands for its fullest manifestation the most complete nature. The more we are men, the greater our capacity for Christianity.

This being so, how strange it is to find men who modestly assume the character of Christian philosophers; and yet when the word self-denial, mortification, or asceticism is pronounced in their presence, they startle like one who is about to be exorcised! An ascetic, in their courteous language, is "a miserable victim of a falsely interpreted religion, starved and withered in delusion." Miserable victim indeed, if the highest purposes of life are, to gratify our animal instincts and give one's self up to ease and self-indulgence! Deluded certainly, if it were our belief, as it was that the heathen, that the grossest indulgence of sensual passions is a part of religious worship! On such a theory, an ascetic is unquestionably a miserable victim! But do these men really fancy that all that lies beyond their mental conceptions is delusion, like the Chinese, who look upon all that come from beyond the limits of their country as barbarians? Can they never learn the simple truth, that the practice of self-denial and kindred virtues, will always correspond in degree to one's conception of the dignity of the human soul, and the greatness of its destiny. Or are they cognizant of this truth, but pusillanimous like the **Jews, who** conjured up to their imaginations, "monsters of the sons of Enac, of the giant kind," **being** too cowardly to face the dangers and conquer the enemies which stood between them and the possession of "the land flowing with milk and honey"?

Strange indeed it is, that these self-called liberal Christians are not liberal enough to allow men, who have higher aims than the indulgence of sensual propensity and appetite, to live the life they like! If a man abstains from eating meat, why not let him, if he likes, eat fish? **If another is bent on** practising entire abstinence, why not allow him **to** fast? If another fancies he will improve by scourging himself, why not let him whip his body? If another takes the notion to shave his crown and walk with uncovered feet, **wherein is he to be blamed?** If another seeks the desert, or ensconces himself in a cave, what commandment does he break? What is there criminal in these actions, that there should be displayed so much spleen against those who live in this way? Christ was born in a stable, he fasted forty days and forty nights in the desert, and often had not a stone to rest his weary head upon. Daniel fed upon pulse, and gained both wisdom and health. The Baptist fed upon honey and locusts, and "*there has not risen among those that are born of women a greater than John the Baptist.*"

These men were in pursuit of a great object. You perhaps don't perceive it! It is because the object which they aimed at does not lie within your range of vision, but above it. They were hungering and thirsting after the beauty of holiness. This was the great aim of their lives, and they followed it up like men in earnest.

> "Life was to them a battle-field,
> Their hearts a holy land."

Be true to thyself, O friend; and learn to "*let every one abound in his own sense,*" and in thy liberality, "*let all the spirits praise the Lord.*"

Meanwhile the practice of these virtues richly repays the soul. They restore to the soul her true and perfect liberty. Is this not a great boon? Suppose that a queen was torn from her throne by a band of ruffians, and being stripped of her royal robes, was clothed in rags, and thrown into a dark and loathsome prison. Abuse and contempt are heaped upon her, putrid meat and filthy water are given to her for food and drink. Her cries are unheeded, and often she meditates an escape, but the sight of the cold and massive walls around her shake and overpower her resolutions. Enfeebled and exhausted, she finally relapses into indifference and despair. Now a slight but strange noise reaches her ears. It grows louder and louder. She listens attentively, and to her quick ears the sounds seems to come like blows **struck** upon her prison walls. **They come nearer** and grow louder; **the iron** bars of her cell give way under them; **friends** enter and her chains are broken. **She** steps forth free, breathes once more the fresh air, sees the fair world around her, and she is replaced with increased splendor and dignity upon her throne. **Can you not** easily imagine that every stroke she heard given against her prison walls, must have sent a thrill of joy through her whole frame? What language can express the gratitude which filled her heart toward her deliverers? And this is simply the picture of a soul which has been subject to the demands of its lower appetites and passions, and has been freed by the practice of self-denial. For what prison walls are so strong as the tyranny of passion over the soul? What degradation is equal to that of a Christian enslaved by vice? What food is so loathsome to the body as lust and sensuality must be to a soul made for wisdom and virtue? What comparison is there between the relief felt at escaping from a material prison to the liberation of the soul from the fetters of sin, free to breathe the pure air of angels, and feed on celestial joys. Oh! blessed virtue of Penance which emancipates the soul, and restores that image of God which is stamped upon it, to its original beauty and splendor!

Besides, penance renders a man invincible against his spiritual foes. The mortified man is like a horse in the open fields. You may approach him with a halter in hand, and almost lay your hands upon him, but he easily escapes your grasp. So the devil may approach a man who has gained mastery over his appetites and inordinate affections, with his temptations, and the opportunity of committing sin ready at hand, but he has no power to capture or bind him. But the self-indulgent man has not the moral life to resist, nor the strength to escape; he is easily led into sin and made the slave of the devil. The mortified man is like a flower which draws nothing but its necessary nourishment from the earth, and that through a slender stem, while it opens wide its bosom to the light and air of heaven; so he, by self-denial, has narrowed all those avenues of his soul which lie earthward, while his whole mind is open to the contemplation of God, and his heart is filled with the taste of His sweetness.

Moreover, it renders the practice of prayer easy. All the irregular movements of our lower nature being subdued, the soul thus disengaged is able to think steadfastly on God, and attend to his inspiration, according to those words of the divine Spouse in Scripture: "*I will lead her into the solitude, and will speak to her heart, and she shall sing there as in the days of her youth.*"* According to the

* Osee ii., 14.

experience of all spiritual men, the spirit of prayer can only spring from mortification. "Give more study to mortification," says Lewis da Ponte, "than to contemplation, for an unmortified person seeks after the spirit of prayer and cannot find it, whilst prayer itself seeks the man who is truly mortified, and knows how to find him." Saint Ignatius once heard one say in the praise of a great servant of God: "He is a great man of prayer." The saint replied, "No, he is a man of great mortification." And on another occasion he remarked, that "a quarter of an hour spent in prayer is sufficient to unite a mortified man closely to God; whereas an unmortified man would not obtain this in two hours." "He who does not live according to the corruption of the senses," says St. John of the Cross, "has the consolation to see all the operations of the powers of his soul tend to the contemplation of God as to their centre."

Finally, it fills the soul with spiritual consolations, according to the words of Holy Scripture. "*Who is this that cometh up from the desert flowing with delights, leaning upon her* *beloved?*"* While the heart is disturbed with irregular affections and filled with inordinate love for created things, divine love cannot enter it. The desert of which Solomon speaks in the passage just quoted, is produced in the soul by the renunciation and mortification of the irregular movements of the sensual appetites, and the soul then goes forth to meet the celestial spouse; and as all obstacles to his love are removed, she is filled with his divine consolation. And thus supported by her Beloved, the practice of every virtue becomes easy. "*Whilst my heart was dilated with thy consolations, I ran in the way of thy commandments.*"† Oh, blessed penance, which recovers for the soul its supreme good, and gives it here a foretaste of Paradise!

Let us, then, enter upon the duties of Lent with the conviction of their necessity and their high importance. Let us manfully conquer all our repugnances to the works of penance enjoined by Holy Church; for every act of self-denial and mortification of sensuality will open avenues of true spiritual joy to the soul. Let us pass through this holy season with sincerity

* Cant. viii., 5. † Psalm cxviii.

and confidence, practising all its requirements, that it may be said of us also, "*Who is this that cometh up from the desert, flowing with delights, leaning on her beloved?*" For only those who take part in the penances of Lent can share in the joys of Easter.

www.ingramcontent.com/pod-product-compliance
Lightning Source LLC
Chambersburg PA
CBHW030001240426
43672CB00007B/782